Quarreling with God

Mystic Rebel Poems of the Dervishes of Turkey

Quarreling with God

Mystic Rebel Poems of the Dervishes of Turkey

Translated & Compiled by
Jennifer Ferraro
with Latif Bolat

White Cloud Press
Ashland, Oregon

White Cloud Press
PO Box 3400
Ashland, Oregon 97520
www.whitecloudpress.com

Printed in Malaysia
First edition: 2007

Cover design by David Ruppe, Impact Publications
Interior design by Christy Collins

Library of Congress Cataloging-in-Publication Data

Quarreling with God : mystic rebel poems of the dervishes of Turkey
/ translated and compiled by Jennifer Ferraro with Latif Bolat. -- 1st
ed.
     p. cm.
 Includes bibliographical references.
 ISBN-13: 978-1-883991-68-5 (pbk.)
 1. Sufi poetry, Turkish--Translations into English. 2. Sufi poetry. I.
Ferraro, Jennifer, 1974- II. Bolat, Latif.
 PL235Q37 2007
 894'.351308--dc22
                              2006032691

Contents

Acknowledgements

We would like to thank the following individuals for their assistance, guidance, feedback, and support throughout the process of making this book: David Fideler, Sondra Tudor, Kyce Bello, Heather Ferraro, Pasha Hogan, Abi-Ru Shirzan (Debra Bunch Ghosh), Prof. Talat Halman, Neil Douglass-Klotz, Kabir Helminski, Prof. Kemal Silay, Gary Kliewer and the team at White Cloud, and to audience members around the world who have been the first to hear and experience these poems in concert and provide the inspiration for this project. Many thanks to our families, friends, and fellow travelers on the path. Special thanks to our teachers for illumination of the bountiful path of Sufism in the present day, and to all the dervishes past and present who seek the truth of Love within the heart of humanity. We would also like to thank the Turkish Ministry of Culture for support of this translation project.

To the Reader: A Note about Terminology

Since the original language of these poems was Ottoman Turkish (translated into modern Turkish in our sources) which included many Arabic and Persian terms, for the most part we have used the accepted standard English equivalents for common Arabic Islamic terms. In cases where the transliteration is of a specifically Turkish name or term, we have used the closest English equivalent in terms of pronunciation.

In addition, many different terms exist which describe the One Reality or Divine Being that is God/Allah. In order to be inclusive, and because different terms tend to emphasize different aspects or manifestations of that One Reality, we have used various words and phrases, always capitalized, throughout the text. These include the Divine, the Divine Being, the One, the One Being, Reality, Truth, Love, Absolute Reality, the All, God, Allah and the Friend. We hope the reader will not be distracted by this and will supply his or her own preferred terminology.

Introduction

Turkey's long tradition of mystical and lyrical poetry and folk songs remains vibrant and evident in everyday life. To foreigners from the West, it frequently seems that everyone in Turkey can sing and play music. Often at gatherings someone—perhaps a rug salesperson or a student—will spontaneously pick up a *saz* (a lute-like instrument) and sing while others join in on *bendir*, *darabuka*, spoons, or voice so harmoniously that the music sounds rehearsed. Typically Turks, even youngsters wearing rock n' roll t-shirts, know a repertoire of folk songs and can sing lyrics of poems by Yunus Emre, Turkey's most beloved ancient mystical folk poet. Such mystical folk songs are called *ilahi's*, hymns to the Divine, or *nefes'es*, literally meaning "breaths." The poems of Turkey's unique mystical traditions have been arranged for music over hundreds of years in the haunting musical scales called *maqams*. The folk traditions in Turkey often overlap with the mystic or Sufi dervish traditions since many of the songs derive from poet troubadours (*ashiks*) who traveled the Sufi path to Truth.

Poetry is often the preferred genre for mystical wisdom across spiritual traditions, and the poetry of Sufism may well attain the pinnacle of poetry's potential as a force for human awakening. Sufism is the mystical or gnostic path within Islam, which, like any mystical tradition, is concerned with the inner experience of religion rather than with its external forms and dogma. The Sufi path, in essence, is the soul's journey from separation back to union with God, the Beloved. In orthodox Islam, the human being is entirely submissive to God, who remains unknowable, all-powerful and distant (similar to orthodox Christianity or Judaism). In Sufism, the Divine Being (God) is not separate from the human being but rather exists in the human heart. This is expressed beautifully in a *hadith qudsi* (extra-Qur'anic Prophetic tradition) that is very important to Sufism: "Heaven and Earth do not contain me, but the heart of my faithful servant contains me."

The Sufi seeks to remember the Divine Being, the Beloved, in every moment and to dispel the illusion of separateness. The relationship with God is that of lover and Beloved. While the lover begins the journey in the pain of separation, and through many stages reaches the bliss of union, the Beloved was ever present within the heart through every stage of the journey. The idea that the heart must be broken or emptied, and the ego (*nafs*) purified so that the Beloved can reside there, is also found in the Qur'an: "Wherever there is a ruin, there is hope for a treasure— / why do you not seek the treasure of God in the wasted heart?" (Sura 18). This process of emptying and breaking the ego and heart often opens the way for the experience of all-embracing unity from which the poet's ecstatic utterance is born. It is in moments of such all-embracing unity that the Sufi realizes the ultimate oneness of Love, the lover (the human being) and the Beloved (God/Allah).

Sufi poetry addresses the Divine Being using the language of love in romantic expressions that can seem shocking due to their passion and playfulness. For the mystic in Sufism, desire is seen not as negative in itself but rather as pointing the way to the desired oneness with the Beloved, our source and destiny. In fact, our longing for the Beloved is the proof of the infinite longing of the Beloved for us. The sooner we realize this, the sooner we leave the reflection of the moon in the pool we have been content with and seek the moon itself—Absolute Reality.

The term "dervish" refers to one in a state of spiritual poverty—and while the first dervishes were in fact wandering ascetics who chose poverty, the term's deeper meaning refers to a nature that is "empty of desires." Dervishes, the "lovers" of God, seek to remember God in each moment, to polish the mirror of the heart so that it may reflect more and more of the light of the Beloved. Through "dying before death," purifying and transforming the limited ego, the "lover" leaves himself and finds the Beloved in his own heart and in everything he sees. It is a paradoxical process of surrender and opening of the heart—the "throne" of the Beloved—so that it can include all beings and states of being in unity. The idea that the Divine Being experiences itself through the mirror of human beings runs throughout much Sufi poetry. Thus, Sufism is the "Path of Love." It is love which burns through the mind's objections and veils and opens the heart to receive the intoxicating vision of Divine Reality.

This book is the natural outgrowth of musical performances of the traditional Turkish Sufi songs and poems we have given throughout the United States and elsewhere. After our performances, audience members often asked how to find translations of the songs, many of which are now translated here for the first time. These requests, as well as the great popularity of the mystical Sufi poetry of Mevlana Jelaluddin Rumi, suggested that it was time to introduce these beloved Sufi poets of Turkey to Western readers.

The verses of only one of these poets, Yunus Emre, have been previously translated in book form and available in America. Yunus Emre, a contemporary of Rumi, is Turkey's best-known mystic folk poet. Like Mevlana Jelaluddin Rumi, Yunus Emre was influenced by the culture and vast landscape of Anatolia. Rumi's poetry, however, reflects urban life in Konya in the thirteenth-century and the poetic styles of the Turkish Selçuk court. It was composed primarily in Persian. The poetry in this volume, in contrast, reflects the orientation of rural village life. It uses simple fresh imagery. Furthermore, it was written in Turkish, which was not considered a refined language during the Selçuk and Ottoman times. Although the poems in this book may not have the linguistic intricacy of Rumi's more classical Sufi poems, they have a candor, simplicity, and vigor due to their grounding in the real physical world of the poet. Some of the poets, including Yunus Emre are thought to have been illiterate (*ummi*). The poems spoke to the uneducated as well as to the educated.

The power in these dervish poems comes in large part from the fact that they were *meant to be sung*. They were composed to swiftly and easily penetrate the hearts of the common people, illiterate or literate. Their mystical teachings were meant to liberate and illuminate humanity and to guide sincere seekers on the path to Truth.

Further, the poems in this volume transmit powerful messages about the social, political, and religious conditions in Turkey during the Selçuk era and the Ottoman Empire. Many of the dervishes—followers of the Sufi path who proclaimed the unity of the human being and the Divine Being—were persecuted, exiled or even killed by the religious authorities of their day (see biographies of Nesimi, Pir Sultan Abdal, Niyazi Mısri). Despite such fates (or perhaps because of them), they became popular voices in the folk poetry of Turkey. Religious orthodoxy, hypocrisy, and intolerance were their targets; uncompromising devotion to truth and mystical love were their aims. These dervishes did not accept the notion of a distant God who judges human beings. Instead, they "quarreled" with God, expressing an intimacy and knowledge that was scandalous at the time. This poetry, full of mystical love and yet crying out against injustice, offers a valuable perspective for our contemporary world polarized by religious intolerance and zealotry. These poems demonstrate an uncompromising devotion to the faith that comes from the inner experience of religion. They robustly sing of how Love dissolves barriers and overcomes social and religious conventions of all kinds.

As translators, we strove to balance faithfulness to the original meaning of the poems with the rhythmic lyricism and playfulness characteristic of the genre. We hope that these lovers of truth will reach across the centuries to awaken today's spiritual travelers with the fragrance of their mystical intimacy.

The Bektashi Dervish Poets of Turkey

Most of the poets in this collection are considered part of the Alevi-Bektashi lineage of Sufi dervishes, which holds a unique place in Turkish mysticism and society. Among Sufi orders, the Bektashis are viewed as both the most unorthodox yet most Turkish of the Sufi orders. One can find elements of pre-Islamic shamanistic beliefs in their teachings and practices. Like most other Shiite dervish orders, they trace their lineage to Ali, Prophet Muhammad's son-in-law. This linkage is central in understanding the content and imagery of their poems. The Sufi aims to become the perfect human being, a mirror of the Divine Being. Ali reflects the essence of the Divine Being in humanity. He is considered by the Bektashis to be equal to Muhammad in importance, forming a trinity of Allah-Muhammad-Ali. Human beings cannot attain the prophethood of Muhammad, but they can aspire to become like Ali, a perfect human being (*insan-i-kamil*) and a servant of the Divine Truth.

The Bektashi Order of Dervishes was founded in the thirteenth-century by Haji Bektash Veli, its patron saint, and during the Ottoman Empire grew to become one of the largest Sufi brotherhoods in Anatolia and the Balkans. The order has always been closely linked with Turkish village life and customs. The Bektashi had strong ties with the Janissaries, a powerful military order in Turkey until 1826, when they were wiped out by Sultan Mahmud II. The Janissaries were essential in the expansion of the Ottoman Empire at its beginning, due to their extraordinary fighting abilities and devotion to the faith. However, due to Sunni domination of the empire in later years and the increasing drive toward modernization, the relationship between the sultans and the Janissaries deteriorated. The Bektashi Order was effectively wiped out in 1826, with most of its leaders being killed or sent into exile and the administration of their lodges given over to Sunni Naqshbandi sheikhs. It was at this time that the "secretiveness" that is a characteristic of the order became more prominent, as Bektashis were forced underground. While by the late 1800s there was a resurfacing of the order and some Bektashi books were published in Turkey, the abolishment of all dervish orders in 1925 made Bektashism an invisible, though palpable, presence in Turkey.

Despite the secrecy of the Bektashis' practices, the poems themselves have been sung in Turkey for centuries. Their endurance and popularity attests to the deep impact the dervish orders and their mystical beliefs have had on the Turkish psyche. Further, the poems represent a controversial and often suppressed tradition of Sufism. Perhaps because Bektashism has always been outside the establishment, and has no unified doctrinal system but incorporates a diverse tapestry of radical and heterodox beliefs, it has continued as a subtle and irrepressible presence in Turkey and the Balkans to this day.

The Alevi-Bektashi poets passed down their verses in the form of devotional folk songs called *nefes'es* which were sung in dervish ceremonies in the *tekkes* (dervish lodges) and have since been preserved in the folk music of Turkey. Some also published their work in written form in *divans* (collections), some of which survive to this day. Often poets of the Bektashi Order were folk heroes with extensive influence in the political and religious life of the times (see biographies of Pir Sultan Abdal and Shah Hatayi). The order's doctrines and rituals were frequently shrouded in mystery and concealed from Sunni religious authorities. Its dervishes (avowed adherents of the Sufi path) were often passionately committed to revealing truths that challenged injustice, hypocrisy, narrow-mindedness, and intolerance. As a result, some dervishes were exiled, some were persecuted, and some were killed because of the perceived threat they posed to the interests of the Sunni-dominated Ottoman Empire. Because the dervish orders played such a significant role in Turkish society, a dervish could win the allegiance of the Turkish people and muster popular support. This base of power threatened the authorities. Fifteenth-century dervish Shah Hatayi even rose to become the ruler of Iran during the Safavid dynasty. Other dervishes, such as Yunus Emre, lived a humble existence characterized by devotion to the sheikh, or *murshid*, and purificatory and spiritual practices undertaken at the *tekke*, or dervish lodge. Dervish orders flourished in Turkey until 1925, when they were banned by the founding father of modern Turkey, Atatürk, whose sweeping reforms made the nation a secular state.

A Social, Political and Spiritual Challenge

Of all the Sufi orders, the Bektashi has always granted the most equality and opportunity for women. They undergo the same initiation ceremony and participate equally with men in gatherings. This alone has led to suspicions and accusations of immorality, since such a custom would have been (and still is) unorthodox in the Islamic world. Another practice that sets the Bektashi apart from other Sufi orders is the occasional use of wine (forbidden in Islam) in their rituals. Historically, these factors led the religious establishment and even more conservative Sufi orders to suspect them of heresy. Scholars such as John Kingsley Birge[1] have pointed out that not all Bektashi groups permitted the use of alcohol. Several poems included here, however, take issue with the religious doctrine that prohibits intoxicating substances. It is well known that most Sufi poetry refers to wine metaphorically—as in the "wine of Love," referring to intoxication with the Divine Being. Certain poems, though, seem to "push the envelope" about what is considered lawful or permissible in spiritual life. Nesimi wrote in the fifteenth-century, for instance, "Sometimes I study life's

---

[1] John Kingsley Birge, *The Bektashi Order of Dervishes* (London: Luzac Oriental, 1994).

meaning in the holy books, / Sometimes I go to the tavern and get drunk." The tavern and drunkenness may be standard symbols for the Sufi's divine intoxication rather than literal drunkenness; Edip Harabi's "Hey pious one, / Show some reverence to wine!" in the nineteenth century is less certainly symbolic.

Annemarie Schimmel[2] reminds us that for most Sufi mystics, rather than rejecting Islamic law (*sharia*) proclaimed in the Qur'an and perfected by the Prophet, they interiorized it, going beyond but not necessarily bypassing the requirements of ritual prayer, fasting, and pilgrimage. The profound understanding of the Qur'an and Islamic law was the ground out of which Sufi mystics grew. While behavior and interpretation may have varied among the more heterodox Sufi mystics, most can be assumed to have had thorough knowledge of the Qur'an, to have loved and exalted the Prophet Muhammad, and to have engaged in prayer, fasting, and pilgrimage intensively as part of the spiritual path.

The most contentious aspect of these Sufis even today, however, is their willingness to proclaim the unity of the human being and the Divine Being. Repeatedly their poems reveal striking examples of the non-dual realization of mystical union. As the sixteenth-century poet Muhittin Abdal writes:

> Muhittin proclaims the Truth a spectator.
> God is simply everywhere if you're willing to see.
> What is the hidden, what is the apparent—
> What a human being is, now I know.

Similarly, in the eighteenth-century Agahi Dede writes:

> Agahi and the Divine Light shine the same
> For the candle's flame
> and the moth who plunges in it
> are the same.

In addition to expressing the unity of the human being and the Divine Being, many poems are adamant about the unified trinity of Allah-Muhammad-Ali. Since each individual is capable of becoming a perfect human being, each of us is implicitly included

---

[2] Annemarie Schimmel, *Mystical Dimensions of Islam* (Chapel Hill, NC: University of North Carolina Press, 1975).

in that trinity. Ali is considered to be the way and goal, and is addressed as the Beloved in some poems. With Ali as intermediary, the distance between humans and God is bridged, an idea expressed in a popular *nefes* by Hilmi Dede Baba:

> I held the mirror to my face—Ali appeared before my eyes;
> When I gazed into my deepest being—Ali appeared before my eyes.

Yet a human who seeks the truth must still commit to following the path—being a faithful student of a master (*murshid*) or sheikh who has attained the truth, becoming purified in the "fires of love;" surrendering the false ego (*nafs*), learning humility and poverty, and practicing spiritual friendship.

The most provocative characteristic of the mystic dervish poets in this collection is their tendency to challenge, or quarrel with, traditional religious beliefs and conventions. They quarrel with God, and in doing so, criticize the emphasis on outer piety instead of the faith that comes from direct spiritual realization. All of these poets were devoted to Prophet Muhammad and his family and knew the Qur'an intimately, but their interpretations of Qur'anic scripture and Islam differed from those of the Sunni establishment, and even from the more conservative Sufi dervish orders. For example, the sixteenth-century poet Azmi humorously challenges Allah with the words:

> You deal death to every living creature;
> Are you a wheeler-dealer?

In actuality, the poet is taking issue with the limited conceptions of Allah and drawing out their absurdity. He is intimate enough with his Beloved to address Him like this.

These poets quarrel with orthodox believers who express dualistic notions of sin and piety. Nesimi writes:

> The wine of this love is a sin, the orthodox think—
> The sin is mine. I fill my glass and drink.
> What of it?

They quarrel with other seekers, beseeching them not to stray from the path of truth in response to criticism, persecution, or illusion. Pir Sultan Abdal counsels:

O dear lover, the testing and challenges on the Way—
You couldn't take it.
Didn't I tell you?

Above all, these poets challenge *us*, the listeners and readers, to reach the state of awareness beyond dualities, to attain the intoxication with the Divine Being that comes from surrendering the self entirely.

The Bektashi dervish poets of Turkey present a provocative and challenging synthesis of mysticism with social and political engagement and resistance. They renounced materialism and worldly preoccupation. Turkish scholars call some of these mystic poets "men of action." They were not cloistered away from society but immersed in everyday life with jobs and families. Some, such as Shah Hatayi and Pir Sultan Abdal, were even political leaders. Some poets followed the path of the legendary Sufi martyr Mansur al-Hallaj, who affirmed in the tenth-century "An-al-Haqq" ("I am Truth /God") and was executed for heresy. Nesimi refused to retract his mystical statements and was skinned alive as punishment. In their lives as in their poems, profound insights into the nature of Truth were accompanied by action.

Their poems' persistent and often humorous rebellion against traditional interpretations of religious law and scripture enriches our understanding of mystical thought and practice within the Islamic world. Their poems beg us to re-examine not only what is essential to the spiritual path but also what is the relationship between religious forms and inmost mystical realization.

Prologue

The Thirteenth-Century: A Master Saint Arises

Just what was it about the thirteenth century that was able to produce some of the world's greatest mystics in a short span of time and relatively small geographic region? Amazingly, Mevlana Jelaluddin Rumi, Yunus Emre, and Haji Bektash Veli all arose out of the social and religious conditions of thirteenth-century Anatolia. While no comprehensive or scholarly discussion is intended here, a brief introduction to the times and the spiritual figure who established the Bektashi lineage of dervishes in Turkey is in order.[3]

John Kingsley Birge, the eminent scholar on Bektashis whose groundbreaking book[4] remains the most in-depth study of the order, describes the conditions that helped to create the mystical and secret religious fraternities in Turkey. Ordinary people in Anatolia during the Selçuk era endured constant warfare, constantly changing political alignments, and waves of immigration, particularly from Central Asia. This instability created the overall climate in which mystical teachings flourished. Due to the Crusades, Christianity and Islam had been in close contact for over a hundred years. In fact, on the frontiers and among the common people, Christian, Islamic, Greek, and shamanic pagan elements blended with Islam to create a uniquely Turkish synthesis of beliefs and customs.

Many of the rural folk and peasantry were isolated and alienated from the central government and "high" culture that developed around the capital cities. The elite and educated learned Persian, the language of literature and arts, and Arabic, the language of Islam. In the cities the tendency toward orthodoxy increased. Among the masses, though, religious expression was growing less orthodox and more heretical as the disillusionment with the central government grew. A tendency toward heterodoxy grew more pronounced.

---

[3] For an in-depth treatment of the subject, please see the seminal study by John Kingsley Birge, as well as other texts provided in the bibliography.
[4] Birge, 1994.

Following the Mongolian invasions, Turkmen "Babas" (spiritual fathers) started immigrating into Anatolia from Central Asia. These wandering dervishes and mystics were especially influential among the frontier peoples. They spoke Turkish, not Persian or Arabic. Furthermore, their teachings incorporated and preserved many of the old pre-Islamic shamanistic customs. Followers of the great twelfth-century Turkish mystic Ahmet Yesevi, their philosophy was anti-materialist and socially and politically active in character. Birge suggests that their philosophy may have appealed to the masses for several reasons. On the one hand, the lack of political security in the thirteenth-century may have led to a widespread sense of insecurity and a conviction that life was unsettlingly transitory. Leaders desired conquest, especially in the name of religion, and desired plunder from the conquered. In these bloodthirsty times, people sought meaning and a more spiritual outlook on life. In response, two spiritual orders were formed in Turkey which would have a great influence over the entire Ottoman era. The Mevlevis (founded by Mevlana Jelaluddin Rumi) were an urban dervish order closely tied to spiritual literature written in Persian. On the other hand, the Bektashis were closely related to Turkish village life and the military. The literature of the Bektashis was in the Turkish vernacular of the common people. The founder of the Bektashis, and the order's patron saint, was a wandering Turkmen Baba named Haji Bektash Veli.

Much about the life of Haji Bektash Veli is unknown or shrouded in legend. We know that he came from Khorasan, like many mystics who settled in Anatolia. Khorasan, which is in the region of what is today eastern Iran and western Afghanistan, was the home of many mystics. Located on the ancient Silk Road, it was at the crossroads of Muslim, Buddhist, Hindu, Christian, and Zoroastrian traditions. Haji Bektash was believed to be descended from Ali, and was in the spiritual lineage of Ahmet Yesevi of Turkestan. After journeying for a period of years to Mecca, Damascus, and Baghdad, Haji Bektash settled in Turkey. In a century of uncertainty and foment, Haji Bektash Veli gained popularity among the rural and uneducated peoples and gained a reputation, among both Christians and Muslims, of having miraculous powers. The stories of his miracles and feats, as told in the *Vilayetname of Haji*

Bektash (Book of Sainthood), continue as familiar folklore and are a matter of accepted belief to the faithful.

To understand the differences between Haji Bektash Veli and Mevlana Jelaluddin Rumi in the Turkish psyche, visiting the tomb of each is instructive. Mevlana's tomb in Konya is one of the highlights of a trip to Turkey for many Westerners. The entire complex around the tomb daily fills with tourists from all over the world. Devout Muslims journey there. So do spiritual seekers of diverse religious backgrounds, impassioned by the intoxicating mystical poetry. Nevertheless, the atmosphere is serious and reverential. Religious artifacts are under glass, museum-like, and the visitor is moved through the rooms in a sea of humanity. The experience is replete with picture taking and loud conversations.

The Haji Bektash Tekke in the Cappadochia region of Turkey, in sharp contrast, feels almost deserted. Stillness pervades the area. On our visit to the tekke, an elderly woman was devoutly praying, sitting on the floor right next to the tomb. Before she left she kissed the tomb and the door frame many times and appeared to be in a state of heightened emotion. If Rumi is an exalted and revered master to most Turks, Haji Bektash is more like a beloved uncle—he's one of the people, an approachable saint. The devoted can show him love and bring their requests and prayers to him. There is no need for formality or ceremoniousness. Devotion to Bektash is simple, straightforward and heartfelt. The Principles of the Bektashi Path, as set forth by Haji Bektash Veli, reflect the same simplicity and love:

Principles of the Bektashi Path

1. Seek and find.
2. Whatever you do, do it for the Truth.
3. There exists in you a "there is" to replace every "there isn't."
4. He who walks the Path never tires.
5. There is no rank or station higher than the Friend's heart.
6. The one who is wise but doesn't share his wisdom is ignorant.
7. To the ignorant, abandoning what is no longer needed is death; to the wise it is birth.

8. There is no repentance of repentance.

9. Let your heart, your hand, and your table be open to others.

10. Look for the key to all within your deepest being.

11. Whatever you seek, look within.

12. Do not forget your enemy is also a human being.

13. The beauty of human beings is the beauty of their words.

14. If the path appears dark, know that the veil is in your own eyes.

15. All blessings upon the one who overlooks another's shortcomings.

16. All blessings upon the one who makes a secret of secrets.

17. The Word is Truth.

18. Do not hurt others, even if you are hurt.

19. Hand-in-hand, hand in Truth.

20. One hour of meditation is better than seventy years of piety.

Other sayings attributed to Haji Bektash Veli include: "The best book of all is the human being," and "Educate your women—a nation that doesn't educate its women cannot progress." If one visits the small Turkish village of Haçibektaş in August, one will witness the annual international commemoration ceremonies for Haji Bektash Veli and get a sense of the order's living presence and traditions.

While not all of the dervish poets in this collection are Bektashis, all were influenced by the legacy of this spiritual order. The subject matters, styles, and attitudes prevalent in their mystic hymns show the debts owed to Haji Bektash. All the poets here were involved, to some degree, with the Sufi dervish orders that have been on Turkish soil and in the Turkish psyche since the thirteenth-century. Like branches of the same tree, the beliefs of these dervishes vary slightly. The core spiritual tenets and orientation, and the mystic realization behind those beliefs, however, is the same. There is a

remarkable continuity of expression throughout the poems. In the section of this book entitled *A Key to the Sacred Universe of the Poems*, we discuss some of the common philosophical, Qur'anic, and doctrinal concepts that aid in understanding the poetry's Sufism in general and Bektashism in particular. It is only fitting that we start the journey through eight centuries of Turkish mystic folk wisdom with the root of the tree where it all started, with the father of the "breaths" of centuries, Haji Bektash Veli.

Haji Bektash Veli (13th c.)

My riches, properties and assets all stayed behind.
My son, my daughter, my relatives, all stayed behind.
But there was one friend who never left my side—
Whatever I did for the Beloved, stayed with me.

Knowledge is the true Master that illuminates the darkness;
Ignorance and heedlessness darken human beings.
The sun of happiness that shines out of the soul
        doesn't rise from East or West.
It rises out of pure faith.

I saw the Friend in my dream and I asked,
"Which path will lead me to you?"
He declared, "You'll find me when you
        abandon you."

O You, you're always repenting something.
Tell me, when will you repent of your repenting?

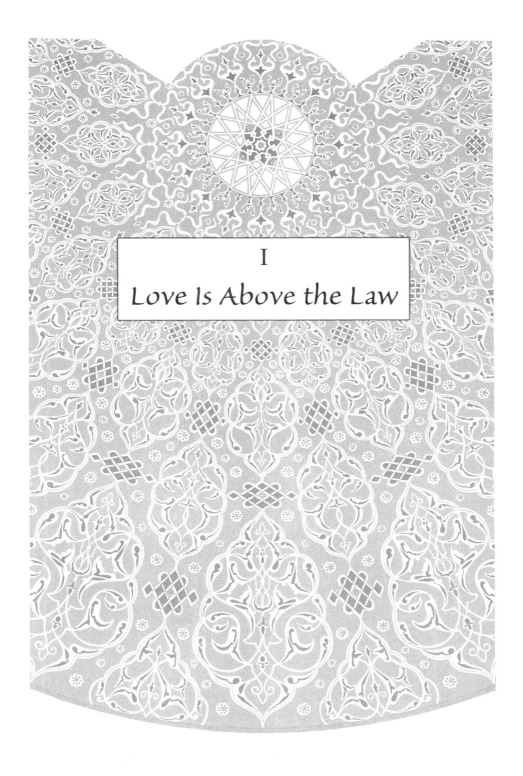

I

Love Is Above the Law

Love Is Above the Law

The poems in this chapter communicate directly and intimately with the Divine Being, the Beloved. They explore the mysteries of love and denounce anything that stands between the soul and the Beloved, including religious laws and narrow interpretations of ritual, scripture, and pious behavior. When love has become everything, when the Beloved is recognized as both the seeker and the sought, one's relationship to outer ritual and forms of worship changes.

Yunus says, "I have no desire but for You" and rejects Paradise as a "reward" for his faith. Nesimi traverses the levels of immanence and transcendence fluidly, telling us, "Sometimes I rise up and watch the universe from above,/sometimes I go down to earth and lose myself in love—/what of it?" Self is obliterated in the longing for union with one's Beloved. There is no room for anything other than "You" in the I-Thou relationship. The secret intimacy of communion with one's Beloved cannot be fathomed by another. Nesimi ends one poem admonishing those who would gossip and trivialize his love, "Whether we get along or not,/my Beloved is mine—/What of it?" Pir Sultan Abdal shows that separation and union are two sides of the same unity when he writes, "Faraway and near to me, in the horizon and in my home,/Wherever I look, my beloved Ali himself is there."

Love can cause sweet chaos to ensue, breaking down barriers and boundaries both social and spiritual. There is a famous Sufi story of the sheikh who falls in love with a Christian girl and leaves his loyal students, his religion, and even his dignity in the dust. He falls into complete and utter despair and humiliation in his devotion to this young girl. While he is eventually redeemed and recovers from his anguished state, his "fall" is not condemned and viewed as sinful weakness. Instead, the experience is seen as part of the human-divine mystery of love, wherein we must often be "cooked" and suffer great indignities, disappointments, and anguish, as well as ecstasy, in the path of transformation from lovers into Love itself.

Nesimi (15ᵗʰ c.)

What of It?

I myself took up the cloak of blame;
I smashed the bottle of honor and virtue on a stone.
    What of it?

Sometimes I rise up and watch the universe from above.
Sometimes I go down to earth and lose myself in love.
    What of it?

Sometimes I study life's meaning in the holy books.
Sometimes I go to the tavern and get drunk.
    What of it?

Sometimes I enter my garden to pick roses for my darling;
I grew those roses and I gathered them.
    What of it?

The wine of this love is a sin, the orthodox think—
The sin is mine. I fill my glass and drink,
    What of it?

The pious bow to the niche in the mosque.
I bow at the Beloved's doorstep, pressing my face up close.
    What of it?

My enemy says loving beauty is sinful.
I love my Beloved so I'll gladly pay that price.
    What of it?

They ask Nesimi,
are you and your Beloved getting along?
Whether we get along or not, my Beloved is mine.
    What of it?

Yunus Emre (13th c.)

Let Them Have Paradise

My eyes exist to see You.
My hands exist to reach You.
Today I set my life on your Path—
       Tomorrow I will find You.

Today I set my life on your Path,
so tomorrow you may know my worth;
Don't give me Paradise as reward for my faith—
       I have no desire to go.

The place you call Paradise
for which every good believer strives
is but a house of beautiful women to the wise—
       I have no desire to embrace them.

You gave me a son and a daughter
who've brought me every pleasure;
Even for them I have no more desire—
       All my desire is for You.

Give all that to the orthodox believers—
They are the ones who want Your favors.
I have no desire for home or possessions either—
       I have no desire but for You.

Yunus misses You terribly.
       Show him that You miss him too.

If Your way is not to torture,
show some mercy so he can reach You.

Ümmi Sinan (16th c.)

With a Thousand Remedies, What Would I Do?

In this world I have one affliction.
    With a thousand remedies,
        what would I do?

I have but one darling in my heart.
    With a thousand lives
        what would I do?

Since I attained to this loving,
    my life is a sacrifice to the Friend.
    My abode is the traceless.
        With some corner in space
        what would I do?

If love doesn't overtake me
    and scorch me in its flames—
    If the fire doesn't cook me—
        with name and fame,
        what would I do?

I desire to renounce all
but the pain he gives me.
    If he doesn't give it, even with both worlds—
        What would I do?

When love finally found me
I moaned and cried for days.
    I found what I was searching for.
        With the little that remains,
        what would I do?

I became the lover of Love,
I became one with the One;
      I became Moses and the mountain—
         with God's distance,
         what would I do?

I was heedless.
it came to me as disgrace and loneliness.
My own Beloved taught me what I know.
        With the sciences of transience,
           what would I do?

Through this affection
I became wealthy in Emptiness.
        Holy pilgrimage, alms-giving, reputation,
        with these gifts,
          what would I do?

The life of Ümmi Sinan
        is a living burning testament of Love.
        He is a faithful servant—
          with rebellion,
          what would he do?

Niyazi Mısri (17th c.)

Let's Whirl, Lovers

My soul wants to give up all else but this—
    Let's whirl, lovers, remembering the Beloved.

My heart wants to renounce all worldly things—
    Let's renounce, lovers, remembering the Beloved.

What does the lover care about the world?
    He is a master of burning and suffering in love
It's his desire for union that makes him revolve—

    Let's whirl, lovers, remembering the Beloved.

Don't reproach me for my condition—
    Don't blame this prayer's ceaseless motion—
I found the remedy for my suffering—

    Let's whirl, lovers, remembering the Beloved.

I was initiated and entered the meeting house of Love.
    I became Mansur* in the gallows of "I am God"—
Niyazi burns now in the fires of love—

    Let's whirl, lovers, remembering the Beloved.

---

*Mansur al-Hallaj, martyred for proclaiming "An-al-Haqq" (I am God/ Truth).

Aşık Veysel (20th c.)

If This Love Did Not Exist

Your beauty wouldn't be worth a penny
    if my love for You did not exist.
Never would I find a place of rest
    if this throne in my soul did not exist.

If I wrote my troubles out, I'd run out of ink.
    My love for you is the only cure.
Your name would never have spread so far
    if love in lovers' hearts did not exist.

For one person to read, another must write.
    Who among us can untie this knot?
The lamb might even befriend the wolf
    if opposite purposes did not exist.

Your beautiful face would not be seen,
    this love would never take shape in my breast,
the rose would have no special place
    if love and the lover did not exist.

I received this suffering from Your hand.
    It turns out to be the taste of the world.
Veysel's name wouldn't even be remembered
    if his love for You did not exist.

Niyazi Mısri (17th c.)

Now No Trace Remains

I thought that in this whole world
        no beloved for me remained.

Then I left myself.
        Now no stranger in this world remains.

I used to see in every object a thorn
        but never a rose—

the universe became a rose garden.
        Not a single thorn remains.

Day and night my heart
        was moaning "Ahhh!"

I don't know how it happened—
        now no "Ahhh" remains.

Duality went, Unity came.
        I met with the Friend in private;

The multitude left, the One came.
        Only the One remains.

Religion, piety, custom, reputation—
        these used to matter greatly to me.

O Niyazi—what has happened to you?
        No trace of religion now remains.

Hayri (19th c.)

Hayri Would Say Much More

If only
      a fire existed in my heart
to match the darkness of her hair.

If only
      that fire might be a lamp
to light the gathering of lovers.

If only
      for a little allowance from Love,
I'd smash the palace of perfection.

If only
      to drink the wine of love with you,
I'd let the tavern doors slam closed upon me.

If only
      the lasso of the wise ones were about my neck,
my soul would stop wandering in this crazy valley.

If only
      he could see her face for just one day,
Majnun would leave his moaning madness.

      What might have happened?
What might have happened?

If only
      the wine bearer would bring us some wine,
and if only
      the goblet might become a mountain to shield us—

      Hayri would say so much more of this love.

Pir Sultan Abdal (16th c.)

A Beauty in Union Station

When I reached the station of union,
     I saw a beauty there
whose lips were sweet,
        whose presence sweeter.

I asked around and found
     that there were many lovers.
Like me, many moaning from separation
     were there.

In my dreams and imaginings
     I see his* beauty divine;
My soul in heavenly drunkenness
       touches God's throne.

Faraway and near to me,
     in the horizon and in my home,
Wherever I look, my beloved Ali himself
     is there.

Sometimes he lives in my garden
     and appears as the rose.
Sometimes he's in my heart
       and speaks the Truth he knows;

Sometimes he's a guest in my soul's house and then goes;
In his bag of tricks, many ruses for his lovers
     he keeps there.

Thank heaven I reached the station
     of this love;
I took pleasure in Friendship's
     fertile grove;

Into the gathering of the realized
     I fell from above
and now the noose around my neck
     is there.

I, Pir Sultan, adore
     a heart-ravishing beauty.
He is the rarest jewel in the whole universe,
     easily,

if you can bear with his kindness
     and coyness
          alternately.
Tell me, is there another of his kind
     anywhere?

---

* We chose to use the pronoun "he" in this poem because the referent is
Ali in the refrain; however, in the original Turkish, the pronoun is gender
neutral.

Nesimi (14th c.)

She Answered No

My hawk-eyed one just woke from sleep.
Are you drunk? I said.
She answered, *No, no.*

Her creamy hands are hennaed every shade.
Is there a celebration? I said.
She answered, *No, no.*

I said, *Why are you smiling?*
It is my coquetry, she said.
I said, *Is it your eyebrows?*—
It is my eyes, she said.
I said, *Did the moon just rise?*
It is my face, she said.
Give me your face so I can kiss it, I said.
She answered, *No, no.*

I said, *There is light*
In my glance, she said.
I said, *My sins are many*
In my heart, she said.
I said, *Is it moonlight?*
In my bosom, she said.
Let me see, I said.
She answered, *No, no.*

I said, *Is it your homeland?*
It is my province, she said.
I said, *Is it a nightingale?*
It is my rose, she said.
I said, *Nesimi is the king*
He is my slave, she said.

Would you sell him? I said.
She answered, *No, no.*

Seyyid Seyfullah Nizamoğlu (17ᵗʰ c.)

Why Should I Not Whirl?

My heart is sick with love;
Tell me, why should I not whirl?

My duty is to suffer and complain;
Tell me, why should I not whirl?

The fire of love consumes my breast;
All who pass me think me mad;
The moon and the sun are both whirling.

Tell me, why should I not whirl?

Come, erase the doubt from your heart;
Why deny its meaning, if you have faith?
Even the angels have been seen whirling.

Tell me, why should I not whirl?

We are the ones saved by the Beloved's grace;
We are the ones devout in prayer;
If pilgrims around the Kaaba whirl,

Tell me, why should I not whirl?

Only with faith can you discern the secret;
The blind forever miss the path;
The heavens themselves are ever-whirling.

Tell me, why should I not whirl?

The wind swirls, the ocean roars.
The river rushes down the mountain.
The water, overflowing, swirls and whirls.

Tell me, why should I not whirl?

Seyyid Nizamoğlu, be strong.
Without faith, doubt only multiplies.
From infinity to eternity, it is our destiny:

Tell me, why should I not whirl?

Kul Himmet (16th c.)

No Ordinary Goods

I made my intellect a friend to me
      But my heart wouldn't accept the advice he gave;
The heart has a big sack it carries with it
      When I stuffed the world in, it didn't fill it.

We are obliged to accept another's greeting—
      This pen made of luminosity said: *Write!*
It is the Beloved who created this flower's light
      and whoever smells it finds all existence in it.

Don't wander like a vagabond, serve a spiritual master—
      Keep your eyes ever on the path you're on.
Do not set your wares before unworthy ones;
      These are no ordinary goods and you're no seller.

Youth is like the summer, old age like the winter;
      Still, in my heart fresh sorrows enter;
So bow your head and serve the Master
      You'll never reach the goal with the devil's manner.

Kul Himmet has a bouquet of roses in his hand;
      He keeps the name of the Beloved ever on his tongue;
I am in love with a beauty on the path to that One—
      My soul's imagination is her throne.

Hasan Dede (Kul Hasan) (15th–16th c.)

Here Is the News

Eşrefoğlu*, here is the news:
We are the garden and the rose is in us;
We are the servant of the Beloved—

Seventy-two languages are in us.

Is it fair to tire out one who's fair?
To be asking always what's over there?
We should remember and proceed with care—

All four rivers of paradise and this rushing flood are in us.

There are some whose bodies are lovely and strong
but when they do ablutions they get it all wrong.
Our words and deeds are our people's song—

All the responsibility for them is in us.

There is a bee which flies and flits around,
he chooses what skin will be his ground;
Our Beloved escapes from us and flies around—

We are the bee, the honey is in us.

Some are orthodox, others are not;
We are all thankful and give praise to God!
For the crown of the Prophet is what we've got—

His cloak and his shawl are in us.

We are the truth of the gnostic knowers,
The garden of all gardens—its mystic flowers!
Of Hadji Bektash, the skillful dancers—

Good manners, virtue and the Path are in us.

Hasan Dede is just a servant here;
It is the tongue which tells the meanings clear.
The letter *Alif*** is the path to truth, so hear:

How if you seek the *djim*,[+] the *dal* is in us.

---

* Eşrefoğlu: The poet wrote this poem in response to criticism by one of his contemporaries, the sheikh and poet, Eşrefoğlu Rumi.

**Alif: the first letter, the 'A' of Arabic, the straight shape of which represents the oneness of Allah.

[+]Djim, Dal–Letters of the Arabic alphabet.

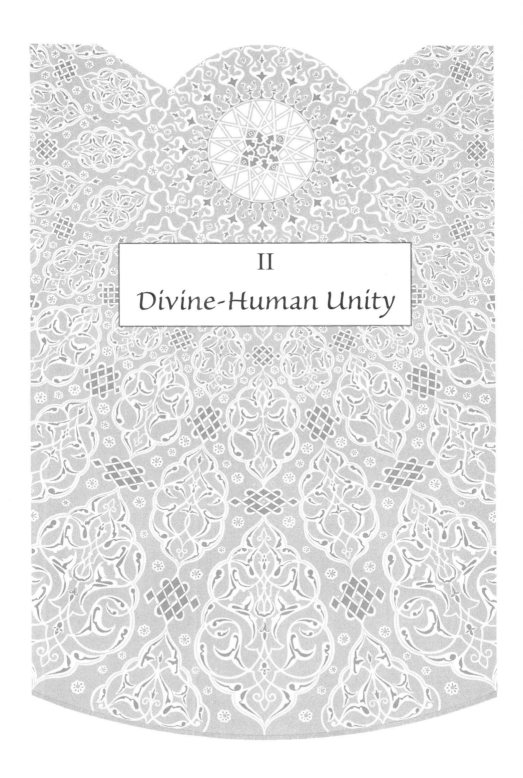

II

Divine-Human Unity

Divine-Human Unity

The poems in this chapter express the oneness of the Divine Being (God/Allah/Reality) and the human being. These poems provide a non-dualistic perspective from which seeming opposites, such as faith and blasphemy, sin and virtue, being and non-being, are realized ultimately as the same Truth. The only way a thing can be known is through its opposite. We need darkness in order to know light; existence can only be known through non-existence. We experience duality and separateness from the One Being because we have not conquered self enough to perceive and develop the Divine in our own hearts. In Sufism, it is Love (*ashk*) that can pierce the veil of duality and reveal the oneness of existence. The burning spark of love is in us because it is the very nature of Reality. It is a passionate longing of the heart to return to its source. Agahi Dede, in the opening poem of this chapter, attests that there can be no such thing as "that which is God" and "that which is not God." What we consider with our dualistic consciousness to be sacred and profane are both the One Reality, but the One Reality must grant such a realization of unity. Without it, prayers and rituals are meaningless.

One of the most distinctive features of Bektashi poetry is its use of wit and humor. The poets often poke fun at others and themselves. This delightful quality allows the illustration of paradoxical and profound truths without becoming too serious or self-righteous. It was against the backdrop of religious persecution and cultural suspicion that many of the poems in this tradition were composed. The poets found it amusing to use language which was outwardly shocking, which would stir the wrath of the orthodox, yet whose inner meaning would be understood by the initiated. Sometimes the speaker of the poem is ambiguous. Is the poet writing the imagined words of God, the Beloved, to us? Or is the poet speaking from a transfigured "I" in the sense of Mansur al-Hallaj proclaiming "I am the Truth/God" (thus indicating the existence of human beings in God and God in human beings)? When Kaygusuz Abdal writes, in the fourteenth-century, "I am the infinite, the eternal—/the hidden treasure is in me," in what sense shall we understand this "I"? It is not as easy as saying it is Kaygusuz assuming his own divinity. Nor can we simply affirm that he is speaking as the One Being who is separate and beyond the reality of Kaygusuz. The poem could radically alter perceptions of reality and the relationship of the human being to the Absolute Truth if used as a meditation, a kind of koan.

Many of these poems exist on several levels simultaneously. Total submission in faith, "I" submitting to "Thou," may alternate in a poem with non-dual realization of unity. Sometimes the two occur simultaneously. In a charming variation on this theme, Hilmi Dede Baba finds his beloved Ali each time he gazes into the mirror, and finds him in everything else he sees, as well. As Seyyid Seyfullah Nizamoğlu says of such sweet and total confusion, "I am amazed, I am amazed!"

Agahi Dede (18ᵗʰ c.)

The Tavern and the Temple

O Righteous one,
to me, the tavern and the temple are the same.

The sounds of praying and of drunken revelry
    are the same.

Unless you're granted the taste of unity,
    whether you pray or sit at the tavern

it amounts to the same.

Leave all your hopeless duality.
    Whether I worship or drink it is the same.

I don't care if I live in ruins
    or hold the whole world in my hand.
The wise and the crazy often look the same.

Don't trade your soul for worldly riches.
    Agahi and the Divine Light shine the same—

    for the candle's flame
and the moth who plunges into it

    are the same.

Kaygusuz Abdal (14th–15th c.)

The Hidden Treasure Is In Me

The ocean, the endless sky,
the quarry and the gems are in me.

Open your eyes, look carefully:

both worlds are in me.

The spirit and the body,
the proof and the evidence,

both profit and loss—

the whole marketplace is in me.

I am the purpose of mankind,
the whirling movement of the earth;

I am the school and the knowledge—

the seal of completion is in me.

I am the Muslim. I am the Christian.
I am the place they both consider holy.

I am the crucified savior, the good and the evil—

whatever *is*—is in me.

I am the Infinite, the Eternal;
I am the wealthy and the poor;

I am the rememberer and what is remembered—

Faith and faithlessness are in me.
I am the idol that is worshipped,
        the Kaaba* and the sacred relic—

the purpose of human beings
        and all that comes with them

        is in me.

I am the light particle and the sun itself,
        the hidden and the seen;

I am everything existing under its rays—

        Lover and Beloved are in me.

I am Kaygusuz Abdal, the soul in everyone.

        I am the infinite and the eternal.

The hidden treasure is in me.

---

* Kaaba: the most sacred Muslim pilgrim shrine in Mecca, believed to have
been given by Gabriel to Abraham; Muslims turn in its direction when
praying.

Aşık Veysel (20th c.)

There You Are

I hide Your beauty in my eye;
> Whatever I look at,
>> There You are.

I hide Your presence in my heart;
> How could a stranger live there?
>> There You are.

You are my foundation and my all;
> My intimate one and the word on my tongue;
You bring the greeting from my darling one;
> Within that greeting,
>> There You are.

All the blossoms and tender leaves
> They hide their beauty in reds and greens;
In night's darkness and the dawn's first beams.
> As each one awakens,
>> There You are.

You are the one who made creation,
> who gave life and strength to every being.
There is no ending except for You
> I believe and accept what I am seeing:
>> There You are.

The flute moans "Huuu" in ecstacy
> The waves are roaring, the seas are rushing,
The sun appears to veil the stars
> In its rays' vast shining,
>> There You are.

You are the one who makes Veysel speak;
　　You are the tree and I am your leaf.
The unconscious fly right by what they seek.
　　In both the fruit and seed,
　　　　There You are.

Yunus Emre (13th c.)

Who Can Know My Mysteries?

I am the infinite, the eternal.
      I am the one who gives life to the soul.
For those bewildered I am a cure.
      The rescuer and remedy—it is me.

I am the one who stands solid as a tree
      Who can know my mysteries?
How can those without soul-eyes see?
      The one who enters souls— is me.

At the creation of the earth I appeared
      With just one glance I brought perfect order.
I built an inn of welcome from His power
      and laid the foundation for love. It was me.

I made the flatness of the plains
      and pressed the earthen mountains into forms.
Like a tent flap I stretched the skies
      and the whole earth became beauty. It was me.

It is I who created harmony among men.
      It is I who wrote the scriptures with my pen.
Black letters on white paper and then
      even the Book which He wrote—it is me, me.

It is I who reached union with the Friend.
      It is I who followed His orders to the end.
I am the gardener who sculpts the land
      and puts the world in perfect order—I.

It is I who comes when the Light arrives
     Illuminating the earth and the soul's eye.
When the sea is rough and surf is high
     It is I who guides the ships to safety, I.
It is not Yunus saying all this.
     The One is speaking with my lips.
For the faithless, ignorance is bliss.
     Where time begins and ends—I.

Edip Harabi (19th–20th c.)

Before the Universe Existed

Long before Allah and the universe existed,
      we created both and announced it to all beings—
when there was no appropriate dwelling place for the Truth,
      we invited him into our house and nurtured him.

He didn't have a name yet;
      Let alone name, he didn't have a shape;
he didn't have an appearance or a dress—
      We gave him an image and made him human.

Once his being and identity were known,
      we uttered *BE* and made the very sky.
Together with him, we created the whole universe
      and made known his deepest qualities.

We built the sky and ground in seven layers.
      The universe was completed in six days.
We created all the creatures in the universe
      giving them fruit and grain.

We made up Paradise from absolutely nothing—
      and adorned the virgins and beauties with jewels*.
We made happy all the nations of the world
      with all the usual promises.

We dug a very deep pit and called it "Hell,"
      covering it with so many words!
And over it we built a bridge,
      thinner than a human hair, sharper than a sword.

What we say is irrefutable:
     Birth and death, creation and destruction—
Wherever you look is Absolute Truth;
     We declare: these are the playground of Unity.
Even though creation became through the order *BE*,
     we wandered for a long time, aimlessly—
And finally—the creation of human beings
     just so this huge place wouldn't be left empty.

For those who enter this sublime palace,
     For those who see Truth within the truth
For those in this gathering of Sufis who can handle it—
     Harabi is letting the cat out of the bag.

Hilmi Dede Baba (19th c.)

Ali Appeared Before My Eyes

I held the mirror to my face—
    Ali appeared before my eyes.
I gazed into my deepest being—
    Ali appeared before my eyes.

In Adam and Eve,
    in the All-Knowing God,
within the heavenly spheres—
    Ali appeared before my eyes.

In Noah, confidante of God
    and in His friend Abraham,
in Moses on Mount Sinai—
    Ali appeared before my eyes.

Jesus, the spirit of God
    who is the king of both worlds,
the refuge for the faithful—
    Ali appeared before my eyes.

The infinite, the primordial,
    the hidden and the apparent,
the unblemished, the pure—
    Ali appeared before my eyes.

The soul and the Beloved,
    the religion and the faith,
the Merciful, the Compassionate—
    Ali appeared before my eyes.

Poor Hilmi is your humble servant;
    in everything I see and everything I say
whichever way I turn,
    Ali appears before my eyes.

Muhittin Abdal (16th c.)

What a Human Is, Now I Know

They're always talking about human, human—
    What a human being is, now I know.
They are always discussing heart, the heart—
    What this heart is, now I know.

Within the heart of the believer it was found—
    it wasn't found anywhere outside.
We found it in our own vast selves.
    What faith is, now I know.

This is how they pick the wheat from the chaff,
    and where your words and deeds must speak for you.
This is where the wise ones guide the Path—
    What the essence of this Sufi way is, now I know.

What the pious fearful carry like baggage,
    why they shoot their arrows at the faithful,
What they hide and trumpet in nice language—
    What doubt is, now I know.

Given all these attributes, I became a person.
    Through God's vastness I was forgiven everything.
I found absolute oneness with Reality.
    What the guest is, now I know.

I said to my inner self *Be humble*,
    and the Glorious One showered me in blessings;
There was a sign that seared me in the heart.
    What the proof is, now I know.

Muhittin proclaims the Truth is a spectator.
    God is everywhere if you are willing to see.
What is the hidden, what is the apparent—
    What a human being is, now I know.

Seyyid Seyfullah Nizamoğlu (16ᵗʰ c.)

The Path of Amazement

I cannot say who it is I am.
    I am amazed, I am amazed!

I cannot call this self "myself."
    I am amazed, I am amazed!

Who is in my eyes seeing?
Who is in my heart enduring?
Who is inhaling and exhaling?
    I am amazed, I am amazed!

Who is speaking with my tongue?
Who is listening with my ears?
Who is understanding with my mind?
    I am amazed, I am amazed!

Who is stepping with these feet?
Who is tasting with my mouth?
Who is chewing and who swallowing?
    I am amazed, I am amazed!

Who holds these riches in his hand?
Who is the one throwing them away?
Who is buying and who selling?
    I am amazed, I am amazed!

Why is there life coursing below my skin?
Why are my eyes bloodshot from crying?
Why this religion, why this faith?
    I am amazed, I am amazed!

O Seyyid Nizamoğlu, hear this:
Everything comes from the One.
Abandon yourself to this mighty beauty.
    I am amazed, I am amazed!

Yunus Emre (13th c.)

Yunus Disappeared into This Unity

O Beloved, what is this illness
that has no remedy?
What sort of wound is this
that no bruise appears?

My destitute heart
is always falling in love
and not coming home.

Once in a while he returns to give advice,
but the heart in love never complains.
The one who thinks of himself
is no lover.

In the marketplace of Love,
we are what is sold.
I put my self up for sale each day
but never have a buyer!

The lover pays no attention to worldly rewards,
Free of concern for earth or heaven.
The minaret announces that a lover has died—
Dying belongs to beasts, not to lovers.

O my friend, if you are wise, pursue this path.
Here everything begins and ends.

The door of the mystics
is the door of generosity.
Those who come with sincerity
do not leave with empty hands.

Yunus disappeared into this unity—
and there's no way
he can even think
of coming back.

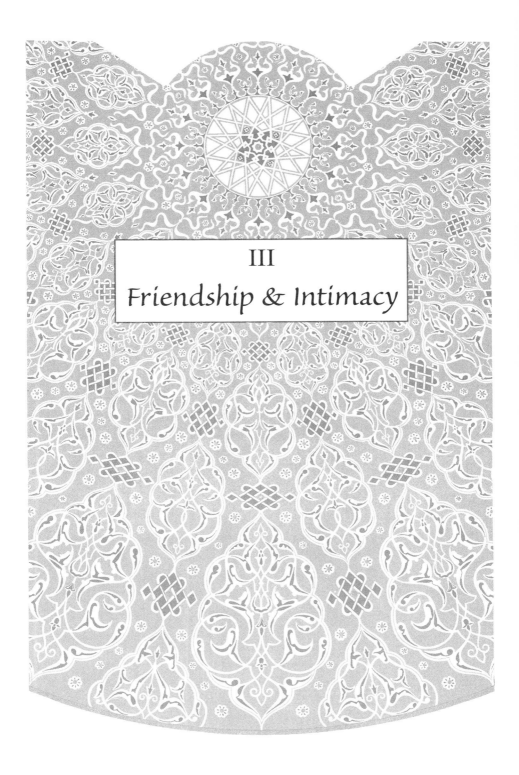

III
Friendship & Intimacy

Friendship & Intimacy

The poems in this chapter describe the important role intimacy plays on the path of love called Sufism. In the original Turkish poems, the word *"Dost"* occurs repeatedly. Although the closest English equivalent is "Friend," it implies an intimate or confidante of the heart and is often used to address the Divine Being. In this context, human friendship is seen as the phenomenon in which the qualities of the Divine Being are made manifest on earth. In friendship and human intimacy we learn how to love. There can be no love for God without also loving human beings: how can one love the ocean but not the drops of water that make up the ocean? Numerous Sufi stories tell of eager students who want to take initiation with a particular spiritual teacher. The teacher asks the student if he has ever been in love. When the student answers no, the teacher tells him to go off and first love a human being and then come back to him for spiritual training. Human relationship is the training ground of the soul, the fire where the heart is honed and transformed. Thus, human connections cannot be avoided or transcended.

The poems in this section express many facets of friendship and intimacy. Nesimi reveals what a radical intimacy with one's own soul looks like, exploring the Qur'anic saying that God is "closer to you than your own jugular vein." He addresses his own soul as "beloved of Allah." Indeed his own soul becomes his beloved, and he includes all parts of his body, heart, and mind in that love. Yunus Emre calls out to the Friend through life and death, from beyond the grave; finally, even his ashes blowing in the wind take up the call. Şair Eşref reveals a paradox: only through surrendering the ego does one meet the Friend. Through giving up existence, one finds true Existence. It is a truth much echoed in Sufi poetry: "I myself was the veil that separated me from You."

Shah Hatayi stresses the importance of devotion to the spiritual teacher. By surrendering to the process of purification in which one is metaphorically threshed, sifted, and stewed in Love's cooking pot, one becomes a nourishment to all, a true friend.

Finally, Ümmi Sinan describes a universe where all has become Love, the rose. The thorn and the blossom—the suffering and pain of separation and the beauty and goodness of union with the Beloved—are both Love. Yet in the last lines of the poem, Sinan tells himself to "heed the mystery" of the nightingale's sorrow for the rose. To realize that Love is everything does not mean one will not suffer or experience separation—for that is the mystery of human relationship, and in a larger sense, of human existence. It is the mystery of loving as human beings.

Nesimi (15th c.)

Welcome My Soul

Welcome, O my soul
that flows
     like water,
welcome.

O sweet-tongued, sugar-lipped,
     soul-stealing
          beauty,
welcome.

Aren't your lips
the mirror
     reflecting all,
and the spirit
     within the saints
that hears the Truth?

That's why, O my beauty,
     the real beauty, my ocean,
          my source
welcome.

Angelic darling,
on your path
     I'd surrender my life.
Beloved of Allah,
since you said
     my flesh is your flesh,
          my blood is your blood,
welcome.

O my face,
my reason, my purpose
    my skin and my heart—
since I found no one else
        suitable to my soul,
welcome.

My beloved came and asked, flirting,
    Dear Nesimi, how are you?
Welcome,
    my soul
    that flows like water,
welcome.

Shah Hatayi (Ismail) (15th c.)

Whoever Gives Up Friendship

In my hidden being a saint told me:
    Whoever gives up Friendship also gives up Truth.

Do not reward such unworthy behavior.
    Whoever gives up Friendship also gives up Truth.

Those who practice love and affection are fitted for God;
    The one who feigns affection is a great dissembler.
His face is stained in the here and hereafter.

    Whoever gives up Friendship also gives up Truth.

Reality is evident within the breath.
    We've dedicated our lives to our darling one.
Down with the one who goes back on his pledge!

    Whoever gives up Friendship also gives up Truth.

Through all the levels and stations of becoming,
    friendship is how God's person becomes known.
Some advice to the faithful of every religion:

    Whoever gives up Friendship also gives up Truth.

The Friendship I'm talking about is of royal line.
    Those without it, what do they know of Truth?
Shah Hatayi's breath* is of the Divine—

    Whoever gives up Friendship also gives up Truth.

---

* The word for breath is *nefes*, which is also the term for the mystic hymns
of this tradition.

Yunus Emre (13th c.)

Calling O Friend, Friend!

My beautiful homeland lay before me
    Let me go there, calling "O Friend, Friend!"
Whoever arrives there stays forever
    Let me stay there, calling "O Friend, Friend!"

When the angel of death grabs me,
My mother and father cannot save me.
So let me ride this wooden horse coffin.
    Let me ride it, calling "O Friend, Friend!"

Let me do the work of solitude
and be a rose in continual blossom—
A nightingale in the Friend's garden.
    Let me sing there, singing "O Friend, Friend!"

Let them take this fabric and make a shroud
to wrap around my shoulders.
Let me shred the clothes of this world
    then climb back in them, calling "O Friend, Friend!"

Let me be like Majnun and journey on,
passing over these mighty mountains.
Let me be a candle melted down
    that as it's melting cries, "O Friend, Friend!"

Let the days pass and the years go by.
Let my grave collapse quickly on me.
Let my flesh become dust out of decay
    which blows in the wind, calling "O Friend, Friend!"

Yunus Emre, keep to your path.
The faithless never enter your state.
Let me be a kingfisher of love on His lake
    that dives in deep, calling "O Friend, Friend!"

Şair Eşref (19th c.)

In the City of the Soul

I traveled through the city of the soul;
    The soul told me all its secrets, whispering.

Some search for a cure for their suffering;
    Lovers look for suffering within the cure.

Find goodness in misfortune, give up searching.
    Can one find much more comfort in a dungeon?

Drink so much of the wine of love
    Your friends will call you crazy in your stammering.

No shame is allowed at this gathering;
    The waters of this spring are cleansing.

When with dervishes, you must become a dervish;
    Only then will you see what riches they're hiding.

Give up your existence on the road to the Friend;
    You'll find the Beloved in that new existing.

O Esref, open your eyes and start remembering—
    In the Holy Book it is written: "Remember me."

Aşık Veysel (20th c.)

O My Saz

When I die, o my *saz**, you must stay in this world.
> but I pray, do not reveal my secrets.
May your tongue stay closed up like a seal.
> Don't cry out like the forlorn nightingale!

I told you all my secret sorrows.
> I struggled and added my voice to yours.
I nurtured you just like a baby in my arms.
> Remember my goodness and don't forget me, please!

When you were a mulberry tree,
> in your branches, were there nightingales?
From which bird did you get this voice of yours?
> Tell me the truth—don't deny your tutors.

You were the one with whom I shared my pain.
> When I laughed or cried you did the same.
Did you receive these words from the sacred Crane?
> Don't strum with your claw and make the bronze strings moan!

When the months and years drag in duress
> Lean against the wall, put on a black dress.
Show the wounds of waiting in your face and flesh.
> Let no one but the Beloved come to tend the mess.

You are the beehive and Veysel the bee.
> We used to moan together and make honey.
I am a human and you a branch of mulberry—
> I don't forget my forbearers. Don't you forget me!

---

* saz: Lute-like folk instrument, sacred to the Alevi-Bektashis.

Shah Hatayi (Ismail) (15th c.)

That's Why I Came

Let's say it with just one breath:
      (How can we ever say it more plain?)
Let's dive into the ocean of love.
      To dive into that ocean,
      that's why I came.

I got closer to my spiritual teacher.
There is nothing left of my heart anymore.
I am a moth, he is the flame.
      To be burnt up in his sun,
      that's why I came.

I am the most humble servant of the Master,
not one with haughty blood in my veins.
I am a nightingale in the gathering of lovers.
      To sing sweetly to you all,
      that's why I came.

In love's harvest I was fully threshed.
I was sifted and then kneaded well.
I went into the cooking pot over high flame.
      To feed and nourish this gathering,
      that's why I came.

Shah Hatayi says these things from his very essence.
There is no contradiction in what he says.
If it is lacking then his essence is to blame.
      To be judged in your gallows willingly,
      that's why I came.

İbrahim (19th c.)

Mercy O Muhammad, Mercy O Ali

When the obvious one asked,
    "Am I not your Lord?"—we answered yes.
Now our thoughts day and night express
        Mercy, O Muhammad, Mercy, O Ali.

I am a servant of the Twelve Imams.
    I sacrifice my head and soul without a qualm.
Love and friendship are what the Truth commands.
        Mercy, O Muhammad, Mercy, O Ali.

Have mercy—our guilt and sin stretch wide.
    "Don't despair, I am Merciful" You said.
You are my protection and refuge—how could I be afraid?
        Mercy, O Muhammad, Mercy, O Ali.

The knowers of the God also know their *nafs*.
    By leaving themselves they always find the Truth.
You see Allah in the light Muhammad casts.
        Mercy, O Muhammad, Mercy O Ali.

You know, my Lord, what is most secret in me.
    My guilt and my rebellion are indescribable.
Day and night I'm repeating constantly
        Mercy, O Muhammad, Mercy, O Ali.

İbrahim is thoroughly bewildered by his Lord.
    Seekers can find him in the city of Reality.
In the face of Muhammad, the Beloved is what we see.
        Mercy, O Muhammad, Mercy, O Ali.

Ümmi Sinan (16th c.)

The Rose

I dreamt I came to a magnificent city
    whose palace was the rose, rose.
The crown and throne of the great sultan,
    his garden and chambers
        were the rose, rose.

Here they buy and sell but roses
    and the roses are the scales they use,
Weighing roses with more roses,
    the marketplace and bazaar
        are all roses, rose.

The white rose and the red rose
    grew coupled in one garden.
Their faces turn as one toward the thorn.
    Both thorn and blossom
        are the rose, rose.

Soil is the rose and stone is the rose,
    withered is the rose, fresh is the rose.
Within the Lord's private gardens
    both slender cypress and old maple
        are the rose, rose.

The rose is turning the waterwheel
    and gets ground between the stones.
The wheel turns round as the water flows.
    Its power and its stillness
        are the rose, rose.

From the rose a tent appears
     filled with an offering of everything.
Its gatekeepers are the holy prophets.
     The bread and the wine they pour
        are the rose, rose.

Oh Ümmi Sinan, heed the mystery
     of the sorrow of nightingale and rose.
Every cry of the forlorn nightingale
       is for the rose, the rose.

Yunus Emre (13th c.)

Let's Take Yunus Emre

Let's be companions, the two of us.
    Let's go to the Friend, my soul.

Let's be close intimates, the two of us.
    Let's go to the Friend, my soul.

Let's go before this life is over,
Before our bodies disappear,
Before enemies come between us—

    Let's go to the Friend, my soul.

Come on, let's go. Don't remain alone.
Let's be a chisel in the Friend's hand.
The only stop will be our sheikh's station.

    Let's go to the Friend, my soul.

Let's leave our towns and cities
and gladly suffer for the Friend.
Let's wrap our arms around our Beloved's waist.

    Let's go to the Friend, my soul.

Let's not be bewildered by the world.
Let's not be cheated by its sudden dying.
Let's not sit together never touching.

    Let's go to the Friend, my soul.

Let's give up this transient world
and fly to the lasting land of the Friend.
Let's give up all the playthings of our *nafs*.

    Let's go to the Friend, my soul.

Be a guide to me on this journey.
Let's set our destination at the Friend,
Not thinking where we begin or end.

    Let's go to the Friend, my soul.

This world isn't everlasting.
With eyes half-open it is tempting.
Be a companion of lovers and a lover.

    Let's go to the Friend, my soul.

Before the news of death reaches us,
Before the hour when he grabs us by the collar,
Before Azrail* makes his sudden move,

    Let's go to the Friend, my soul.

Let's arrive at the Divine Truth
and inquire there about Reality.
    Let's take Yunus Emre with us—

      and go to the Friend, my soul.

---

* Azrail: the angel of death.

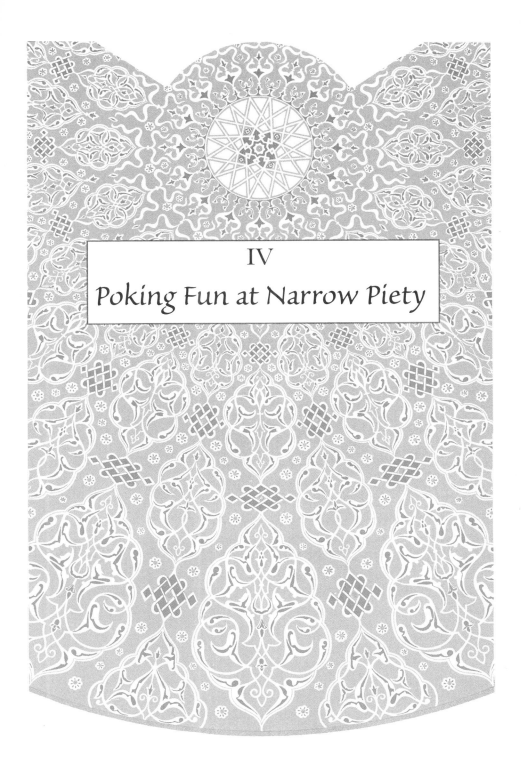

IV
Poking Fun at Narrow Piety

Poking Fun at Narrow Piety

The poems in this chapter boldly challenge limited conceptions of Allah/God as a distant, punitive, reward-bestowing "master architect" whose plan is beyond our comprehension. The narrow interpretations of piety and lawful behavior are addressed passionately. When all is realized to be Truth (God), who can say what is sacred and profane? In the Qur'an it is written, "Whithersoever ye turn there is the face of God." This Divine Omnipresence is not so much an idea to be accepted but a state to be reached as we peel off veil after veil and encounter the One Reality as expressed in the Sufi's most essential zikr, "La ilaha illa Allah" ("There is no god but God" or "Nothing exists but God"). For the true mystic, this encounter can change everything.

In the relationship between lover and Beloved, rules of etiquette may often be suspended. A mystic's prayers might seem crude or irreverent to the average believer, full of challenge, informality, or occasionally, even accusation. Scandalously intimate words may pour forth, bearing the intensity of erotic love or of queries and complaints that may seem blasphemous. Azmi's famous poem, which begins the section, pokes fun at limited conceptions of the Creator and queries Allah about His contradictory and nonsensical arrangements. "I'm not afraid of your hundred thousand hells," Azmi writes. "The name All Compassionate—doesn't that come from you?"

Edip Harabi openly defends the spiritual stature of women and challenges the sexism in traditional religious dogmas, particularly in the sexism evident in the Islam of his time. In a rare poem written with a female persona and signed with a woman's pen name, the speaker of the poem provocatively asks, "O men and knowers of the truth, tell us—/Didn't we give birth to all the masters/who led you on God's way?"

Riza describes his fellow dervishes and lovers of truth as "drunkards," as "regulars" in the tavern of the world where it was "the Beloved's seductive eyes" that taught the mystics what they now know. If these analogies are not daring enough, Edip Harabi actually defends drinking as permitted to spiritual adepts, for whom it has a meaning unknown to others. For those people who have not attained the state of unity, imbibing is a sin. For those who have no sense of duality, no sense of separate existence, how could sin exist, much less accumulate?

Finally, in another famous poem, Kaygusuz Abdal challenges God to pass over the hair-thin bridge that awaits humans on Judgment Day, saying "If you are so brave—/You pass it, O God." God made the world with its good and evil, Kaygusuz asserts, so it is unfair to punish human beings and send them to hell for their failings. Throughout the poem, Kaygusuz appears to criticize and challenge God. At the end, though, he softens and asks his creator to "lift the veil between us" so that he might understand the mystery hidden beneath. His lashing out is only part of a lover's quarrel. Essentially, he wants to be with his Beloved. Closeness and trust allow him transparently to reveal his feelings. Only absolute faith allows the poet to transgress the distance between lover and Beloved. The realization of unity is a kind of wine that intoxicates those normally sane, cautious and respectable. When we seek God's pleasure above all, reputation is not much of a concern. As Shah Hatayi writes, and many Sufis through the ages have affirmed, "Behold, there is faith in blasphemy."

Azmi (16th c.)

Just What Kind of Builder Are You?

You created the earth and sky, human and the *jinn**,
    Are you some master architect, a builder?

You made the moon and sun, the constellations in the sky—
    Are you the maker of these, or just the one who
    makes them shine?

You made rivers run without legs or feet.
    The ground without foundation, the sky without pillars,
You made them stand just like that.
    Are you a prize-winning engineer?

The wind blows without wings or windmills
    Did you make all these mountains with wheelbarrow
    and shovel?
You deal death to every living creature
    You give life and take life—Are you a wheeler-dealer?

You built eight heavens for humankind
    Your name is rather large
So why did you throw Adam out of Paradise?
    Do you need the wheat or what? Are you a farmer?

When Your name is One—You made it a thousand.
    I have never seen such a skillful hand as Yours.
You create green trees and then you dry them up for wood.
    Are you some kind of lumberjack?

You speak to Archangel Gabriel from behind a screen,
    Then you descend to earth to listen to Your news.
What have you to do with the fires of hell?
    Do you own a bath house, are you its coal-stoker?

You hide Yourself and then you watch us.
    You mess with people's minds.
You made that bridge thinner than a human hair.
    Do you have a running river on your property?
Are you a landscaper?

You made this summer worth all the winters
    You made this autumn to balance the spring.
You made a scale with two sides to measure—
    Are you a shop keeper, a vegetable grocer?

It is said that in hell's cauldrons tar is boiling.
    Great entertainments under earth now showing.
It is rumored you keep thousands of dragons—
    Are you an ice cream seller or a snake charmer?

Are you a slave trader that you make some people slaves?
    Are you a teacher that you read and write those books?
Are you a bookkeeper always tallying the figures?
    Are you an accountant or an innkeeper?

I'm not afraid of your hundred thousand hells—
    The name All Compassionate—doesn't that come from You?
Didn't You call Yourself the pardoner of sins?
    Pardon my sins then. Are You a liar?

Would it cost You your reputation to forgive me?
    Even the king would pardon me if he heard my case.
I don't think You'd lose anything from Your treasury.
    Why don't you forgive me? Are you lacking something?

If humans are imperfect, is that really good for your reputation?
    You reside and move in every heart.
You take all these lives and then you return them.
    Are you a caravan driver who picks up and delivers?

You know I am the servant, You are the King.
  You speak through me as I repeat Your name.
You are in my soul as a cherished guest—
  You are my heart's beloved. Do you think You're a
  stranger?

You make me the guide, but You speak through my mouth;
  You negotiate internally with Azmi.
You take dream excursions to the unfathomable peaks.
  Are you the tour guide? Are you the dreamer?

---

*jinn: Beings inhabiting the plane between human and angel, associated
with ideas and inspiration.

Aşık Dertli (18ᵗʰ–19ᵗʰ c.)

Where Is the Devil Here?

This instrument they call the stringed saz
knows neither the holy book nor the judge.
Whoever plays it knows its nature.
Tell me, where exactly is the devil here?

Its strings come from Venice,
Its fingerboard is made of oak.
O shallow servant of Allah,
Tell me, where exactly is the devil here?

Whether or not you do ablutions, this saz won't tell;
Whether or not you do your prayers, this saz won't tell;
Unlike judges, it doesn't know how to scheme for praise.
Tell me, where exactly is the devil here?

Is he inside the saz or outside?
Is he on the peg's handle perhaps?
In the design or on the wooden body?
Tell me, where exactly is the devil here?

The inner chamber is just mulberry,
the frets are only animal guts.
I must ask you, even though it's embarrassing,
Tell me, where exactly is the devil here?

This saz wears no turban, just like Dertli.
It wears no shoes on its feet either.
But that alone doesn't put horns on its head—
Tell me, where exactly is the devil here?

Edip Harabi (19th c.)

They Say We Are Inferior

O Muhammad, they say we are inferior—
     Where is it men got this mistaken idea?
They disgrace the Prophet's family
     with their false claims and blasphemy.

Our mother Eve—is she not a woman?
     Beloved Khatija*—is she not a woman?
The Prophet's daughter, Fatima—is she not a woman?
     Isn't the Qur'an full of praise of them?

These pure consorts of the pure of heart—can they be any less?
     Whoever calls women inferior cannot reach the Truth.
You wouldn't expect these ideas from one who knows.
     Who is it that gave birth to all these prophets of Truth?

God didn't do something absurd in creating us.
     We don't accept being seen as somehow less.
Women raised every saint who has walked the earth—
     I dare you to accept this.

Don't think this world can't exist without men—
     Think about Mother Mary even once:
She gave birth to the glorious Christ, fatherless.

O mankind, we are more courageous than yourself
     because we show respect to you out of love.
We travel together with you on the Path—
     Leave all these empty claims behind.

We may look different from you in our dresses.
In reality we are not trailing behind you.
And we warn you, we don't consider it courageous
to claim we are inferior.

Did Muhammad, the Chosen, come from a lesser being?
Did Ali the valiant, come from a lesser being?
Beware, do not call your mother inferior—
What she prays at night might change your life forever.

Listen carefully to the speech of Zehra.**
O men and knowers of the Truth, tell us:
Didn't we give birth to all the masters
who led you on God's Way?

---

* Khatija: Prophet Muhammad's wife.
** In this nefes the poet speaks as a woman and uses a woman's pen name,
"Zehra," as a signature in the last stanza—a highly unusual occurrence
even in Bektashi literature.

Shah Hatayi (Ismail) (15ᵗʰ c.)

If You Can Distinguish Them, Come Forward

The Truth is locked away in secrecy.
      If you can open it, come forward.
Behold, there is faith in blasphemy—
      If you can distinguish them, come forward.

The gates of Paradise are open.
      You can see it is made of gems and rubies.
The bridge which gets you there is thinner than a hair—
      If you can cross over it, come forward.

Our lives are those of angels
      and our bodies are the purest of the pure.
What I drink is the blood of the lion*—
      If you can drink it too, come forward.

I took advice from my teacher.
      I learned many lessons from my master.
After that I even bound my wings and flew—
      If you can fly, come forward.

I am the rose in the garden.
      I am the nightingale in the sacred gathering.
I am the key to Forty Doors*—
      If you can open them, come forward.

Shah Hatayi is content in what he knows.
      A mystic fog lay over the high mountains.
Here is the Bible, here is the Qur'an—
      If you can distinguish them, come forward.

---

*Ali is considered the lion of Allah.
*Within each of the Four Doors (Gateways) of Islam (*Sharia, Tariqa, Marifa, Haqiqa*) there are ten stations (*maqams*) of maturity on the path to becoming a Perfect Human Being. The saints are those who pass all Forty doors.

Riza (19th–20th c.)

Those Who Make Their Home the Tavern*

In this tavern-like world we are the regulars.
Our zeal for life is pure enjoyment.
Don't blame us,
>   We come from those who closed the book of ambitions;

We have drunk soul-blood in the gathering of knowers.
We found the pleasure of eternity within surrender.
In order to keep our promise on Judgment Day,
>   We come from those who chose what is difficult.

The beloved's seductive eyes taught us what we know,
We wrote poems from her sweet and charming words.
Because we *knew* we had to take a secret way,
>   We come from those who reached the pilgrim's
>   destination.

We have no interest in begging for mercy.
Through knowledge we reached the station of coquetry.
We are quite familiar with those who practice trickery.
>   We come from those who glimpse behind the curtain.

If you are one who knows, then bow before the wise.
Know who you are, instead of showing off.
We pluck more than a single rose from the garden of
Knowledge.
>   We come from those who gather bouquet after bouquet.

O Riza, we are the dervishes, those who have tasted.
We have given up worldly things happily.
We are the drunkards, cleansed of all sorrows.
>   We come from those who make their homes the tavern.

---

*The Turkish original, *meyhane*, means tavern but carries the double meaning
of the dervish lodge, or *tekke*, in poems of this tradition.

Edip Harabi (19th–20th c.)

Show Some Reverence to Wine!

Hey pious one, show some reverence to wine!
    Be truly righteous and stop all this slandering.
It is within the law for adepts to drink wine.
    When we drink, where are the sins accumulating?

It is God's pleasure we wish to gain.
    Your mind has a hard time with this scheme.
Yet it was in the tavern
    that this knowledge was attained.

We become wicks dipped in the oil of Truth.
    We become lit like lamps on the Night of Power.*
We become both the proof and the signpost to Truth.
    But those without vision can never see this far.

If you really are unfaithful, then drinking is a sin.
    You should wait until Paradise for imbibing.
O Harabi, you better not say any more—
    He doesn't know the law's true meaning.

---

*Night of Power: The night when the Qur'an was revealed to Prophet Muhammad.

Seyyid Seyfullah Nizamoğlu (16th c.)

A Single Believer There Isn't

This love is like an ocean;
      A dam containing it
          there isn't.

The secret of guidance is the Qur'an;
      For the one who knows this, shame
          there isn't.

We came from eternity,
      from my king Muhammad-Ali.
For the one who drinks the wine of reality,
      headache or hangover
          there isn't.

If you're in love with the Beloved
      don't believe the wagging tongues
          of strangers;
Be burned up like Abraham was.
      In this rose garden, death
          there isn't.

If you can't give up everything
      then it's best to stay away.
Here we lose our heads without complaint.
      Any regret for the losing
          there isn't.

Those who unite with Truth,
      those who comprehend the Self,
those who die on the path to the Friend,
      Treasure enough to compare to them
          there isn't.

Look at what Mansur has done—
  He brought all these great ones after him;
For those who come down with *An- al- Haqq*
  any cure or remedy
    there isn't.

Seyfullah is drunk with all of this.
  He got his inspiration from his master.
On love-crazed words there are no limits—
  Whatever one says, a single believer
    there isn't.

Kaygusuz Abdal (14th–15th c.)

If You Are So Brave

I have seen what is higher than the highest, Venerable God;

The scholar reads whole sentences—

    You only speak in syllables, O God.

Men are known as "son of so and so…,
but you have neither mother nor father;

    You seem like an illegitimate offshoot, O God

You created the bridge on Judgment Day
and ask your subjects to pass—

It is thinner than a human hair;
Let us step aside right here:

    If you are so brave—
    You pass it, O God.

You created destitute subjects, full of need.
You throw them into this universe

    then You yourself climb away out of reach.

O You who created Kaygusuz Abdal,
come down
    and take the last gulp from this mystery.

Lift the veil between us
    so we can be together as we're knowing this,
      strolling arm and arm.

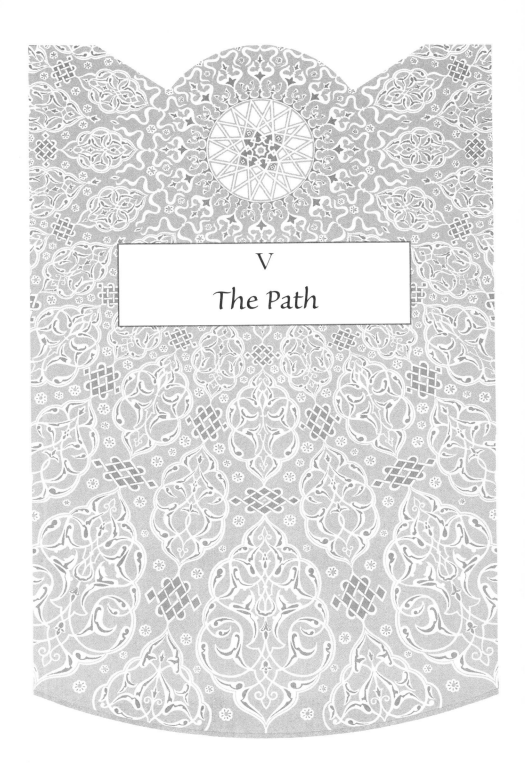

V
The Path

The Path

The poems in this chapter often speak to the demands and re-
nunciations necessary on the spiritual path in order to attain
Truth. "Taking hand" with a spiritual master or guide was the
essential first step on the path. The guide was one who was fully
surrendered to God. Through devotion and surrender to one's
master a student learned how to surrender to God. Because of
the many pitfalls and perils on the spiritual path, the responsibility
of the spiritual teacher to his student (*mureed*) was no small matter.
Mureeds were tested by their masters and underwent many trials
to prove their sincerity, commitment, and dedication. In turn, the
master's job was to guide them safely through the stages of the
path, over many a rough sea, in deep spiritual friendship and constant concern. Taming the *nafs* (limited ego) was the first priority of
the student on the spiritual path, just as one would train an unruly
horse to obey its rider. The mind, heart, and body had to be purified and prepared for spiritual realization. This was accomplished
through training and spiritual practices to deepen and prepare the
student's inner being for grace.

In a rare poem which is kind of a treatise, Aksarayi Şeyh İbrahim
Efendi beautifully elucidates the inner meaning of the Sufi path.
It is a process of not only surrendering one's soul to the Beloved,
but becoming the soul of the Beloved. Yunus Emre attests to the
need for humility above all on the path, and for treading compas-
sionately when it comes to others. He writes humorously, "Even
the one with the long white beard, the one who looks/so wise—/If
he breaks a single heart, why bother going to Mecca?"

Koyunoğlu counsels himself to have the courage to "slip the
noose of Mansur" around his neck—to not retreat from the realization of unity at any cost, even if it endangers his life.

The poems encourage other dervishes (and us as listeners) to
commit unwaveringly to the spiritual path, whose destination is
union with the Beloved. Though the pitfalls and challenges are
many, it is a path of ever-increasing beauty. Aşık Ali Izzet says,
"The eyes that perceive beauty will never suffer." In his final rap-
turous poem, the repetition of the word "beautiful" creates the

state of ecstasy the poem describes. This state is nothing less than full perception of the Divine Beauty in all things: "To love beauty from the depths of one's soul/is beautiful."

Aksarayi Şeyh İbrahim Efendi (17ᵗʰ c.)

The Sufi Way

They say the Sufi way
    is to give one's life away.

The Sufi way is to become a sultan
    on the throne of the soul.

In the station of the Path,
    it is to destroy appearances.
In the station of Reality,
    it is to become a guest
in the innermost palace of the heart.

They say it is to be pure of body,
    the light of the Beloved.
The Sufi way is to gradually take off
    the dress of earth and water.

They say it is to burn up in Love's fire—
The Sufi way is to be utterly inflamed
    with the light of the Beloved.

They say it is to believe and follow the rules—
The Sufi Way is to discover the rules
    of the multitude of heavens.

They say it is to become a medicine for every ailment—
The Sufi Way is to know and become all the secrets
    of creation.

They say it is to destroy the illusion of bodies—
The Sufi Way is to open the secrets of the body
    with the key of the Divine Names.

O Sufi, to comprehend it, one must *be* it.
The one who gets lost in words
    will never *be* their meaning.

They say it is to become the secret of God
    within one's innermost heart—
The Sufi way is to read the outer signs
    and know the inner meanings.

They say it is to be in wonder
    at the greatness of creation—
The Sufi way is to be constantly amazed
    by the nature of Reality.

They say it is to make each heart
    the throne of God—
The Sufi way is to remove all else but God
    from the heart's dwelling.

They say it is to watch over all humanity—
The Sufi way is to cover East and West
    with every breath.

They say it is to shine as brightly as the sun—
The Sufi way is to perceive God
    in every minute thing.

They say it is to be in harmony
    with every kind of person—
The Sufi way is to appear
in a hundred thousand forms daily.

They say it is to be like Solomon
    to the whole universe;
The Sufi way is to understand
    and speak in every language.

They say it is to become an ocean
  from a single drop—
The Sufi way is to make your heart a cellar
  to hold the wine of the Truth.

They say it is to become a human being
  illuminated with the light of Being—
The Sufi way is to destroy Being utterly
  in the light of Non-Being.

They say it is to become a life
  for each particle of life—
The Sufi way is to die a thousand times
  and return to life each moment.

They say it is to become a master
  of wisdom and eternal justice—
The Sufi way is to become an eye
  looking out from every hair.

They say it is to surrender
  your soul to the Beloved—
The Sufi way is to *become*
  the soul of the Beloved.

They say it is the proof
  of Muhammad's message—
The Sufi way, O İbrahim,
  is to embody God
    as one's own self.

Kaygusuz Abdal (14th–15th c.)

Now It's Clearer Than Daylight

The words spoken by the saints—
      That's the Qur'an we read, isn't it?
What the masters of love speak—
      That's a sura of Rahman*, isn't it?

The Divine Truth that created you,
made a mirror of Himself in you,
made Himself manifest in the world like this—
      It's the shape of a human being, isn't it?

For those who listen to the Truth,
and hear it deep in their hearts,
for those who understand what we say—
      One word is proof, isn't it?

If you don't recognize what's real,
if you don't hold it precious in your heart
if you can't distinguish the true from the false—
      that's the only ignorance, isn't it?

O Kaygusuz—what will happen to you?
Be brave and keep traveling this path.
Truth is benevolence to its followers—
      Now it is clearer than daylight, isn't it?

---

*sura of Rahman: The 55th of the 114 suras, or chapters, of the Qur'an.
Rahman (one of the most important Divine Names of Allah) means
Merciful, or Beneficent.

Yunus Emre (13th c.)

One Who Is Real Is Humble

To be real on this path you must be humble—
If you look down at others you'll get pushed down the stairs.

If your heart goes around on high, you fly far from this
path.
There's no use in hiding it—
What's inside always leaks outside.

Even the one with the long white beard, the one who looks
so wise—
If he breaks a single heart, why bother going to Mecca?
If he has no compassion, what's the point?

My heart is the throne of the Beloved,
the Beloved the heart's destiny;
Whoever breaks another's heart will find no homecoming
in this world or any other.

The ones who know say very little
while the beasts are always speaking volumes;
One word is enough for one who knows.

If there is any meaning in the holy books, it is this:
Whatever is good for you, grant it to others too—

Whoever comes to this earth migrates back;
Whoever drinks the wine of love
understands what I say—

Yunus, don't look down at the world in scorn—

Keep your eyes fixed on your Beloved's face,
then you will not see the bridge
on Judgment Day.

Hilmi Dede Baba (19th c.)

Come to the House of the Pir*

A tent is erected
where lovers are slowly cooked—
This stopping place for love addicts
is really a rose garden if you look.

Come to the house of the Pir,
where your inner being is made tender.
It is Love's own fires lighting his burner.

The All-Knowing One lent His own brilliance
to the lover's torch in generosity—
so that even on Judgment Day
that torch would shine and shine.

Hey wine-bearer,
now bring us some of that love-wine.

We will kiss the feet of those drunk with love.

But keep this secret:
what we really worship
is the Beloved's beauty—
Even the ground has ears and can give us away.

Enter the heart of the believer
and bow down there in all directions—
Within one breast, how can you tell
which direction is east or west?

O Hilmi, let the dervish in you be poor and humble.
The Friend is a constant guest
in the houses of the poor.

---

* Pir- spiritual master or teacher.

Koyunoğlu (17th c.)

Look at the Book

We drink from many oceans
　　　just being in love.
It is an army of the realized
　　　who look after the world's needs,
coming with their flag of mercy raised,
　　　running to our rescue.

The wise ones are the hallowed ground
　　　upon which mosque and shrine are built.
They are the rose garden and the glade
　　　overflowing with red roses.

Hey you who are lost,
　　　have you found the Path, finally?
Have you found your inner treasure
　　　and marveled at it endlessly?
If not, heart and soul stay thirsty.

Koyunoğlu, look at the Book—
　　　Slip the noose of Mansur
around your neck.
　　　Like Nesimi, be one with Truth.
It was his skin they flayed, only.

Muhittin Abdal (16th c.)

Just One Taste and They're Addicted

Greetings to those who come from afar,
　　who take this noble path of ours.
Ecstatic lovers and followers of the heart—
　　Those who know the Truth, Bravo!

You commanded it to *BE*—and suddenly it was.
　　The whole universe surrendered to You.
Leaders of men and those lost were conquered.
　　A peace comes over those who serve You.

Walk a straight line, never looking aside—
　　for those who stick to the path don't fade away.
The Divine One pardons and forgives those
　　who only serve Reality.

Come down from those lofty heights;
　　Don't be ashamed—find the lowest patch of dirt;
Feed the hungry, water those who thirst,
　　pay off your debt to those who serve what's true.

Do not feed the wild stallion of anger and wrath.
　　It'll end in growing darkness of heart;
Stamp out the hungry hounds of the *nafs*
　　so your precious body doesn't suffer wounds.

Muhittin Abdal, let there be love* between us;
　　May outsiders never overhear these secrets.
The ignorant would certainly become addicts
　　if they got one taste of this precious fruit.

---

*"Let there be love"— *Ashk Olsun*, a typical dervish greeting.

Shah Hatayi (Ismail) (15th c.)

The Teaching of the Running River

Have you seen the tall mountains topped with snow?
    Already the snow is melting away.
Have you heard the teaching of the running river?
    It stays low to the ground as it flows away.

O Beloved, you are the most able one I see.
    Everywhere I look, you are before me.
You're like a four-cornered tent
    stretching, covering night and day.

All these great birds of knowledge in the sky—
    Why the sun doesn't burn them is a mystery.
The trees which give their fruit to us eternally—
    Even they don't stay long before they're passing away.

Our ocean is so deep you cannot dive it.
    With a thousand words, still few understand it.
You can't leash a person who doesn't want it—
    He'll break the leash and continue on his way.

Shah Hatayi's own heart is in these words—
    But even the eyes of other dervishes he avoids.
His heart is tired, is drunk and sighs—
    For all but his enemies' criticism passes away.

Teslim Abdal (17th c.)

What's the Use?

Heedless one, don't look so surprised.
      You'll die one day like everyone else.
You'll regret one day the things you've done.
      But regrets and repentance—
          What's the use?

You will leave your home for good someday.
      Never stop repeating the word of Truth.
You won't escape the angel of death.
      Taking windy paths to avoid him—
          What's the use?

You say unworthy things and don't retract them.
      You don't distinguish right from wrong.
You eat everything in sight and then are thirsty;
      Even if you had all the oceans to drink from—
          What's the use?

Teslim Abdal piles up a mountain
      made of all his worldly assets.
If it's illusion and falsity that you own—
      Even if you own the entire universe,
          What's the use?

Pir Sultan Abdal (16th c.)

Didn't I Tell You?

O dear lover, the testing and challenges on the Way—
    You couldn't take it.
        Didn't I tell you?

The food of willing surrender on the Path—
    You couldn't digest it.
        Didn't I tell you?

Those who refuse this banquet's fare,
    their eyes are bloodshot in strain and despair.
The breath of revelation falls quickly through air—
    You couldn't listen
        Didn't I tell you?

Let's surface at the very heart of the Path.
    Let's surrender everything for Ali in faith.
Your head on the chopping block of Truth—
    You couldn't lay it.
        Didn't I tell you?

O Pir Sultan, Ali is our king and lord;
    Our tumultuous path ends in God.
The Twelve Imams protect us on this road.
    You couldn't follow.
        Didn't I tell you?

Niyazi Mısri (17th c.)

A Happy Customer You Will Be

One who becomes a lover
  is one who must deeply suffer,
    weeping tears in an endless river—
    A fire raging he will be;

When the hairs of love dampen
  the chest of the lover with grief,
    like Mansur in fateful reunion—
    Destroyed utterly he will be.

Your love makes us *majnun*,
  Your Layla-love of separation
    starts the fires raging in till dawn—
    A pile of ashes we will be.

One who gives up existence
  to journey to the Friend's presence,
    often must cry oneself senseless—
    A gushing spring he will be.

Your love can make a prince a dervish.
  whatever falls into your love may perish.
    Even the throne of a king may vanish—
    Destroyed utterly it will be.

When I became a dervish I left all shame.
  In dervishhood we must renounce that stain;
    Who falls into your love is never shamed again—
    Completely shameless we will be.

In the marketplace of love you exchange
    your life for more than pocket change;
        Give your life and get a Beloved for your pain—
        A happy customer you will be.

You the Sublime Beauty, take this soul—
    Since I saw your face I happily fell;
        Your love has made the world seem small—
        A smaller world forever it will be.

O Niyazi,
    abandon yourself immediately—
        for the one who gives his life willingly—
        Together with his Beloved he will be.

Teslim Abdal (17th c.)

The Job of the Master

The master is one who can resolve all problems;
    What would I do
with one who couldn't help me?

His job is to turn my face toward the Beloved.
    What would I do
with a path that didn't guide me?

The master should ever hold me in his heart;
    Wherever I am, he should be with me.
He should be with me in this world and the other.
    What would I do
with a master who didn't care for me?

The master should know my state of being;
    He should be there to grab my arm if I fall.
When I have a broken heart, he feels it without looking;
    What would I do
with a master who couldn't close his eyes and see?

He should be like the full moon
    that shines in the black sky,
He should reside in both the revealed
    and the hidden;
What would I do
    with a master who stood aside passively?

O Master Ali, this is Teslim Abdal.
    I adore you in this world and the other.
I know you will free me in the courtroom
    on Judgment Day.
What would I do
    with a master who wasn't free?

Aşık Ali Izzet (20th c.)

The Path of the Beautiful

Appreciating beauty is said to be a virtue.
     To see beauty beautifully
          is beautiful.

Those who have a beautiful beloved in Paradise are beautiful.
     To travel the path of beauty
          is beautiful.

The sun rises from the beautiful one's eyebrows.
          The beautiful one's teeth are just like pearls.
     To share beautiful food at Beauty's table
          is beautiful.

To linger with the beautiful one beautifully
     is beautiful—

To write the beautiful name:
     beautiful—

To drink with the beautiful one:
     beautiful—

To kiss the hand of the beautiful one:
     beautiful.

The light drips from the cheeks of the beautiful.
     Honey drips from the lips of the beautiful.

Hold the hand of the beautiful beautifully.
　　To serve the beautiful one
　　　　is beautiful.

The eyes that perceive beauty will never suffer.
　　Who loves beauty may die but will never decay;

Ali Izzet never shies away from beauty—
　　To love beauty from the depths of one's soul
　　　　is beautiful.

A Key to the Sacred Universe of the Poems

In many of the poems, references are made to concepts or terms important to Sufism in general or to Bektashism particularly. While by no means attempting to be exhaustive, this key can provide information that will enrich the understanding of particular poems and open the reader further to their mysteries.

"Am I Not Your Lord?"

This question, often referred to in Bektashi poems, refers to a passage from the Qur'an called the *Elest* (or *Alastu*), which describes the primordial covenant between God and human beings. Before creation, God asked future human beings who were to spring from Adam, "Am I not your Lord?" They answered, "Yes, we witness it." Muslim mystics have attached great importance to the idea of this primordial covenant. For the Bektashi, this has become an allegory for when the consciousness of the Divine Creator and love for that One began in the human heart.

The Perfect Man

This concept was first put forth by the great Sufi philosopher Ibn Arabi and was elaborated on by almost all of the Turkish dervish orders. The general doctrine holds that God created a microcosmic being through whom God's consciousness could be seen by Himself. He is a prototype of the universe and a model for all. However, only the saints and prophets can reach this state. The Bektashis view the cycle of existence as beginning and ending with the Perfect Man (*insan-i kamil*) as the first emanation of Divine Reality. While most Sufis accept Prophet Muhammad as the Perfect Man, the cause as well as the goal of creation, the Bektashis link Ali with Muhammad as one being, and therefore Ali is often revered as the Perfect Man. Bektashis also will tend to esteem their spiritual masters as attaining such a station and in particular poems, speak from a place of attainment of it themselves.

The Master/Spiritual Teacher

Once the wayfarer (*salik*) made up his mind to enter the spiritual path, becoming a *mureed*, he required a guide to lead him through the various stations and model the essence of the path. This was a necessity. Often a *mureed* would search for years all over the Islamic world for a spiritual master whom he could fully trust and give himself to in devotion; Most shaikhs upon meeting a possible disciple would test the newcomer to determine how willing and ready he was to undergo the disciplines and hardships of the path. Once accepted by the shaikh, the shaikh would watch over all aspects of the disciple's spiritual growth and progress. The shaikh's methods and ways of training were different for each *mureed*, according to the particular nature of the *mureed*. Through perfect trust and surrender to the spiritual teacher, the *mureed* learned surrender and perfect trust in God. In Sufism, truths must be experienced directly through living transmission from one heart to another heart. Without a spiritual teacher, progress on the path is hindered. The various terms for the spiritual teacher used in the poems include *Shaikh* or *Pir, Murshid* (Master) and particular to the Bektashi tradition, *Baba* (Father) and *Dede* (Grandfather).

The Four Gateways

One of the key doctrines of the Bektashi Order of dervishes is that Four Gateways comprise the Path: shariat, tariqat, marifat, and haqiqat. *Shariat* refers to the laws of Islam, the outer observances of religion; *Tariqat* refers to the mystical path (gnosis) followed by the Sufis, the inner dimension of religion; *Marifat* refers to attainment of mystic knowledge of God; and finally, *Haqiqat* refers to attaining immediate experience of the Divine Reality. One must pass through each Gateway, which in turn has ten obligations or stages (*maqams*) associated with it, on the path. To pass through all "forty doors" was the goal of the "lover" and the attainment of the Perfect Man, the saint and prophet.

Hurufism

The Hurufis were a particular sect in Shia Islam that had a major influence on Bektashism. In the fourteenth-century, Fazlullah of

Khorasan proclaimed himself a new Prophet after he received a revelation in which God was revealed in the word. He developed theories about letters and their numerical values' interior meanings. He also theorized that God was revealed in the human face as a holy book through which God's secrets could be known. Fazlullah was executed for heresy, but Hurufism became part of Bektashism and influenced most of the Turkish dervish orders in some way. We see this in the emphasis placed on the breaking down of names into letters which have numerical values pointing to hidden meaning. The influence can also be seen in the art work that adorns Bektashi *tekkes* in which the face of Ali and his sons are drawn by combining the letters of their names. One of the most prominent poets in this collection, Nesimi, was a Hurufi.

The Path of Blame/Melamism

The Melami/Melameti Order of dervishes is very connected to the Bektashi Order and influenced several poets in this collection, including Yunus Emre and Aksarayi Şeyh İbrahim Efendi. These dervishes felt that showing one's piety or religious virtue in any way created pride and insincerity in the heart; therefore, they deliberately tried to draw criticism from the world for their unseemly and sometimes outrageous behavior. Though they outwardly took the "path of blame," in secret the dervishes were often extremely pious.

Zikr

Zikr (*dhikr*), is the essential practice and worship of the Sufis. It literally means "remembrance" and entails silent or outward repetition of the name of God, or a sacred formulation of Divine names. It can be done anytime, anywhere. The goal for the Sufi is to remember God in every moment and in every breath, and zikr is the practice most essential to the Sufi in affirming God constantly in one's heart. Zikr ceremonies vary from order to order, but usually involve group chanting or singing, sometimes accompanied by a rhythmic movement of the head and upper body.

Majnun

Majnun is a legendary lover in the literature of the Islamic world, who became demented in his unrequited love for Layla. The name literally means "mad" or "crazy." The story of Layla and Majnun is a common reference in Sufi poetry. Majnun is often a model for the intoxicated and demented lover whose devoted contemplation of the beloved leads to mystical union.

Sema

In many Sufi orders, the practice of sema/sama ("listening") was and is common, but it has never been accepted by more orthodox Sufi orders due to its use of music and sometimes dancing. In this ceremony of worship and remembrance stirring and intoxicating spiritual music often produces in participants a state of ecstasy (*wajd*). The Mevlevi Order founded by Mevlana Jelaluddin Rumi, are well known for their elaborate sema ritual in which white-robed dervishes "whirl" to the accompaniment of hypnotic music. While less elaborate, the Alevi and Bektashi also have ritual sema gatherings, where food and drink are served and dervish trouba-dours playing saz, the sacred stringed instrument, will sing *nefes'es* or *ilahi's* such as those in this book. Symbolic circular dances par-ticular to the Alevi-Bektashis are often danced by men and women at such sacred gatherings and at the annual Haji Bektash Festival in Turkey.

The Twelve Imams

A common subject of praise in Bektashi poems, the Twelve Imams refers to Ali and his descendants, revered by Shiites, who were considered sinless and as having divine authority.

"I was a hidden treasure"

One of the most important reputed sayings of the Prophet (*hadith*) in Sufism is "I was a hidden treasure, and I desired to be known. Therefore I created creation in order that I might know Myself" (*Küntukenz*). This has great significance for most Sufis and Turkish dervish orders. Before creation, God existed as undifferentiated unity. Because of the One Reality's wish to know itself, the world of differentiation and duality was created. However, when human beings can at last see themselves and the universe as not other than Divine Reality but rather as its reflection, then they experience Reality as it is. To the dervish poets, this mystery is contained in the phrase "I was a hidden treasure," and it is referred to and used in many poems.

About the Translations

To translate literally means "to bring across." In order to begin to translate spiritual poetry of one culture and time into another culture in another time, ideally the translator should have fluency on at least four levels: a firm grasp of the syntactic and idiomatic expressions of both languages; facility in the poetic conventions and forms of both languages and cultures; understanding of the spiritual framework and historical/cultural context of both cultures; and an intuitive and experiential grasp of the inner meaning of the poem as a spiritual document, a record of mystical experience in a particular tradition. A tall order, indeed!

My translation partner, Latif Bolat, and I humbly approach this work as artists and travelers on the path of Love. Latif has performed and presented these Turkish Sufi songs to audiences all over the world for twenty years, singing and accompanying himself on the traditional Turkish folk instrument called saz (also called *bağlama*). We have also performed these songs together (I play the frame drum) for audiences internationally. Listeners have often requested translations of the lyrics. The huge body of potent and delightful spiritual literature virtually unknown to the West inspired us to begin work on this book. We completed the majority of translations in southern Turkey during the summer of 2004, immersed in the landscape and folk traditions that have nurtured and influenced the *ashiks* and spiritual poets of Turkey for centuries.

In our collaborative translation effort, Latif provided the literal translations from the Turkish and I created the analogous poem in English. We worked together, back and forth, at every stage. Recognizing the impossibility of conveying the complex cosmological and acoustic dimensions of the original poems, we have chosen "approachable" poems with fewer references and allusions lost to those outside the tradition without extensive explanation. In addition, we chose poems that represented the themes and "moods" of the mystic folk genre as a whole, and included influential dervish poets whose songs are still sung today and whose poems are nearly as cherished as sacred texts. In short, we looked for that elusive quality that meant that either the content or the form could translate well to a modern Western audience.

One of the greatest tasks we faced was to retain the simplicity and conversationality of the original. This was challenging, because a single word or phrase might have many levels of symbolic and spiritual meaning that needed to be conveyed. For instance, one of the terms that is repeated in many of the poems is *Haqq*. This is one of the names of Allah, or God. It literally means Truth, and beyond that, the ultimate Reality. We had to decide whether to use a substitute, another word or phrase whenever *Haqq* appeared, knowing that for Western audiences, there is no precise explanation. In this case, we decided to keep the term, using Truth/God/Reality alternately depending on the particular context. For readers not familiar with Islam or Sufism, the term may challenge. Certain key terms and concepts, such as the Path, the Friend, the Beloved, the Lover and the Tavern, have become familiar in English. The popularity of recent translations of Rumi and other Sufi poets by Coleman Barks, Robert Bly, Kabir Helminski and others has helped in this regard.

Sufi poetry, like other Islamic literature, has always relied upon the turning and elaboration of established metaphors communally and culturally understood: rose, nightingale, garden, lover and Beloved, moth and flame, are a few of these. A poet who built on a complex, historical library of associations and metaphors did not have the need to be completely original in his work. He could use the common language of mystical and romantic experience in fresh ways to add subtle insights or provide an unorthodox interpretation of an idea. A poet could play on a common theme or with a particular metaphor freely. A modern translator schooled in contemporary Western poetics is tempted to add different specific images for these oft-used metaphors weighted with cultural, spiritual, and literary significance. Changing the tropes, however, would change an essential feature of the poetry. We know that there are dimensions of subtle meaning that modern Western readers simply will not get in the translated poetry. Translations are notorious for this loss. However, so much of the beauty and meaning remains that even the worst translation could not seriously damage the poems.

We faced an additional challenge. All of these poems were composed during the Selçuk and Ottoman periods. The Turkish language contained many Persian and Arabic words, which now are obsolete. We had to cross-reference and research many arcane phrases and make some educated choices among meanings. Despite this necessity, we have attempted to keep the translations as close as possible to the original poems.

As the person responsible for conveying the poem in English, I faced many decisions stylistically. Many of the poems containing a refrain naturally called for a particular form. In these poems, I loosely kept the original stanzaic form. Often the form was a modified *ghazal* or a folk form called *koşma*, featuring rhymed syllabic meter. In some poems, I tried to preserve elements of assonance, slant rhyme, and occasionally end rhyme, but I tried to not let stylistic concerns dictate the poem's form. I have attempted to allow the individual poem to determine its container in English. Some poems seemed to call out for a free-verse form—those whose ideas were especially complex or whose rhythmic lines were too dense to re-create in English. Turkish syntax puts the verb at the end of the sentence. This structure assures endless rhyming possibilities and a conceptual fluidity within the poem. Due to the vowel harmony that operates in Turkish, Turkish lyric poems have a unity, fluidity, and lushness of sound that is nearly impossible to achieve in English. However, since most of these poems are indeed songs sung by Sufi dervishes in their rituals and by troubadours in the wider Turkish folk culture, we felt it was important to keep some of the rhythmic song quality and not to work entirely in free verse.

My guiding principle was that if a poem didn't come across in English as a poem, the translation had failed. American audiences arguably "hear" a poem's content best when it is presented to them in free-verse. Coleman Barks' popular free-verse translations of Rumi are an example. We resisted working completely in free verse, however, since the charming character of these poems is so closely tied to song and meter. Line breaks and spacing were used to create the tension that the original rhymed syllabic meter creates. Our titles are meant to be a doorway so that readers can enter each poem. We have arranged the poems thematically into five sections to make them more accessible. It is our hope that these English translations convey a taste of the sacred universe and flavor of the originals. If they do justice to the passionate and profound wisdom that so strongly emanates from these sacred hymns, we have fulfilled the mission we undertook.

Biographical Notes on the Poets

In Turkey, "creative genius" is a less individualistic matter than it seems to be in the West. The folk poets represented in this book composed poems and songs not for fame or personal renown but for spiritual service, out of a concern for fellow human beings. They were villagers from a communal context in which poetry and music were a part of daily life to an extent that we can barely imagine today. Some poets would not use their own names, preferring to borrow the pen name of an admired predecessor to sign their poems. Yunus Emre, so well-known and much beloved, is a case in point. It can be a difficult task to distinguish the real poet from the later imitators who used the pen name. Sorting out accurate biographical information is thus quite a challenge. In some ways, the scanty or confusing information highlights the inherent generosity of this tradition, in which the stream of wisdom and beauty coming through a particular poet mattered more than the poet's own name or fame. The songs belong to all humanity and come from a limitless source. Centuries passing mean nothing, when the waters of wisdom continue to flow from generation to generation, from village to village, on the tongues of bards and within the sacred ceremonies of the dervishes.

We hope these brief biographies (arranged alphabetically) will give the interested reader a foothold from which to explore deeper.

Agahi Dede (18th c.)

Not much is known about Agahi Dede except that he lived during the middle of the eighteenth-century and came from Belgrade in present day Serbia. His real name was apparently Yashar, and he composed his poems primarily in the classical meter called *aruz*.

Aksarayi Şeyh İbrahim Efendi (17th c.)

İbrahim Efendi was the shaikh (spiritual leader) of the Aksarayi Tekke in Istanbul during the seventeenth-century. He was part of the Helveti Order of dervishes, which was one of the most widespread orders (*tariquats*) on Ottoman soil in the seventeenth-century. As a boy, he showed mystical tendencies, growing up in a very spiritual environment. He was greatly influenced by Yunus Emre and in turn, influenced the political figures of his times. He preferred a didactic style in his poems, and during his life wrote four books, including a *divan* (collection of poems) and spiritual treatises on the Sufi path. Another poet in this collection, Riza Tevfik, wrote a long commentary on his poem "The Sufi Way" (see pg. 70).

Aşık Ali Izzet (1902–1981)

The central Turkish city of Sivas, birthplace to many *ashiks* (troubadour poets), was where Aşık Ali Izzet was born in 1902. Before his death in 1981, he became a well-known troubadour. Ali Izzet became an *ashik* at a young age and traveled all over Turkey, from village to village, playing saz and singing songs. He was connected to the Haji Bektash Tekke. Relatively uneducated, he performed at some of Turkey's major cultural institutions during his lifetime and published poems in prominent magazines. He also worked as a saz teacher with Aşık Veysel, another twentieth-century poet in this collection and recorded albums of songs. Some of his songs, such as "I am Majnun and I Saw My Layla," became very popular and have been recorded by other musicians. His poems developed and added to the spiritual themes of Alevi-Bektashi poetry. They responded to the problems of his time. However, he experienced persecution for his left-wing tendencies and died in a shanty house in Ankara in 1981, leaving behind eight volumes of poetry.

Aşık Dertli (1772–1845)

Born in 1772 in the city of Bolu, near Istanbul, Aşık Dertli was one of the most powerful troubadours of his time. His life was difficult and impoverished. When his father died, the wealthy landlord confiscated his father's land and Dertli, whose real name was İbrahim, became a servant. Perhaps his hardships partially account for the great love the common people have for him.

Beginning in the Halveti Order of dervishes, Aşık Dertli later became a Bektashi. His poetry dealt with both spiritual and secular folk themes. He was equally proficient in the folk style, tekke style, and classical style of poetry. His best lyrical poems were written in the "*hece vezni*" style of syllabic meter common in folk songs.When he died in 1845, the people carried his coffin to his birthplace to honor him. Even in the 1960s, his songs could still be heard on the Turkish radio, and some are still recorded. His collection of poems was published both in Ottoman Turkish and in modern Turkish.

Aşık Veysel (1894–1973)

Known all over Turkey, Aşık Veysel was the most beloved troubadour of the century when he died in 1973. He was also blind. Born in Sivas in central Turkey in 1894, he lost his sight to smallpox at age seven. His father encouraged him to learn the saz and recite poems. By the age of twenty, he was a master of poetry and singing and was performing in coffee shops in Ankara. A folklorist who published the most prominent literary magazine in Turkey became interested in Veysel's poems and brought them to a wide audience. Aşık Veysel also made appearances on state radio and television stations. His national reputation enabled him to make his living as a troubadour. He traveled throughout the country. In the style of Yunus Emre, his poems are lyrical and written in the common tongue. They deal not only with spiritual matters but also with daily matters of importance in people's lives. His style was, in its universality, popular in Sunni and Alevi circles, in *tekkes* and in secular communities. Often, his poems dealt with the themes of nature, exile, and mystical experience.

When Aşık Veysel died in 1973, money was raised to build a mausoleum for him in his village. Recently, all his works have been collected in a single volume, entitled (in translation) *May My Friends Remember Me*. Three days before Aşık Veysel died, he was interviewed on Turkish television. The interviewer lamented "You're the last troubadour in a centuries-old chain." Aşık Veysel replied, "Turkish mothers will give birth to many more troubadours. How could I be the last?"

Azmi (16th c.)

A sixteenth-century Bektashi, Azmi challenged the idea that Creation was mechanistic and literal. He also criticized the orthodox views of God. The poem included in this collection, "Just What Kind of Builder Are You?" epitomizes the Bektashi tendency to tease or "quarrel" with God over the absurdity of some eschatological concepts. Poets before Azmi had implied that human beings might be divine, but no one before had put it so radically or confrontationally. The poetry is Azmi's legacy. Few facts about his life survive.

Edip Harabi (1853–?)

Edip Harabi was born in Istanbul in 1853. He saw the fall of the Ottoman Empire and the abolition of the dervish orders in 1924. Recently, Harabi's work has enjoyed a surge of attention and appreciation. His poems and songs are now among those most heard in Bektashi rituals. A Bektashi from the age of seventeen, Harabi was an unwavering supporter of Bektashi causes and philosophies. Harabi nevertheless served as a navy lieutenant.

The pen name "Harabi" means "ruined" or "destroyed." In the turmoil-filled days of WWI, the Sufi orders had come to be in a state of dissolution and this was especially true for the Alevi Orders, which had less protection from the establishment. After Atatürk "dissolved" the dervish orders, traditions were abruptly discontinued. In the chaos, Harabi's work was overlooked for many years.

Harabi's gift for improvisation meant that his poetry was generally recited, not written. Still, upon his death, he left a 600-page *divan* (collection) written in many different styles. The Turkish scholar Özmen comments that in Harabi's poetry, one sees Yunus Emre's themes of love and unity, Nesimi's unwavering nature, Kaygusuz Abdal's satire, and Pir Sultan Abdal's courage. For Harabi, human beings and human qualities manifest the beauty of the Beloved. As part of the Beloved, human beings should not be treated dishonorably. Harabi illuminates the divine in humanity, sometimes satirically and sometimes soft and lovingly. Harabi advocated the equality of men and women and wrote mystical poetry with a woman's name as signature (see "They Say We Are Inferior," pg. 58) His Bektashi poems are supplemented by the many secular poems Harabi wrote during his lifetime.

Hasan Dede (Kul Hasan) (15–16th c.)

Hasan Dede is indisputably one of the most important Bektashi poets. Yet there is little information about his life. Some Bektashis claim that he lies in the grave of a saint named Karpuzu Buyuk Hasan Dede (Big Watermelon) outside Ankara. Hasan Dede wrote his most famous poem, "Here is the News," (p.17) in response to a boast by a member of another dervish order. We also know that Hasan Dede was one of Haji Bektash Veli's *khalifas*, or authorized representatives.

Hayri (1860–1910)

Hayri's real name was Harpütlü Haji Hayri Bey. Born in 1860 in Harput, he studied in religious schools and learned Arabic and Farsi in addition to Turkish. He was apparently a judge in the Ottoman court system. Due to problems with the administration, he moved to Istanbul and remained there until his death in 1910. He translated at least one work from French into Turkish and left a collection of poems called "Memories of My Youth."

Hilmi Dede Baba (1842–1907)

This poet's full name was Mehmet Ali Hilmi Dede Baba. His poems are famous among Bektashis and are widely sung. Born in Istanbul, he was the son of an *imam* (mosque priest). In 1896, he became the *Baba* (spiritual father) at the Azahkulu Sultan Tekke in Istanbul. In the mid-nineteenth century when the Ottoman sultan destroyed the Janissary armies the state began putting Naqshbandi *sheikhs* in place at the Alevi *tekkes*. Hilmi played a great role in stopping the movement to make the dervish *tekkes* Sunni. As a result, during the Turkish liberation after WWII, his *tekke* supported Atatürk against European invasion. He left a collection of poetry in folk and classical styles. He died in 1907.

İbrahim (19th–20th c.)

The real identity of the nineteenth-century Bektashi poet İbrahim is unknown. According to one account, he was the disciple of a Shaikh Munir Baba of Sutluce Bektashi Tekke in Istanbul. He died in 1911. His poem, "Mercy O Muhammad, Mercy O Ali" (pg. 45) implies that God shows Himself in His human creation, and that every path to God must go through human beings.

Kaygusuz Abdal (14th–15th c.)

One of the earliest poets in this collection, Kaygusuz Abdal is also one of the most unusual, provocative, and influential. Inspired by Yunus Emre, he influenced almost all the later Bektashi poets. He was an originator and master of the satirical form in folk poetry, which later became characteristic of the Bektashis. He is known to have lived between 1341 and 1444, and was from Alanya on the Mediterranean. The son of a local king, his given name was Alaeddin Gaybi, and he was involved with the Bektashi *tekke* headed by Abdal Musa, Haji Bektash Veli's successor.

Later, on Abdal Musa's recommendation, Kaygusuz Abdal went to Egypt and opened a *tekke* there. He seems also to have lived near Kerbala and Najaf (in present-day Iraq), made a pilgrimage to Mecca and later died in Egypt. Judging from his poetry, he was educated in the Qur'an and Qur'anic law and mysticism. One story about how he came to his master Abdal Musa is related by Eyuboğlu. One day while hunting, Kaygusuz shot a deer. The arrow went into the deer's back and the deer ran, taking refuge at Abdal Musa's *tekke*. Kaygusuz ran after it, rushing into the *tekke* and demanding that his deer be returned. Abdal Musa pulled the arrow out of his own side, asking, "Is this the arrow you shot?" Kaygusuz fainted on the spot. When he woke, he begged forgiveness and began his spiritual life.

The name of Kaygusuz Abdal has become synonymous with hashish among Bektashis. In fourteenth-century Anatolia, smoking hashish was common in the *tekkes*. In fact, dervishes often wore around their necks coconut shells filled with hashish. Kaygusuz apparently wrote many poems about the virtues of drug-induced states.

Overall, the poetry of Kaygusuz Abdal is distinguished for its strong ties to everyday life. Annemarie Schimmel points out that his poetry is among the most unusual in Sufism. In some poems, he describes his dreams of good food, or his love adventures with a charming youth, or his difficulty in cooking a goose. He also wrote in a form called *tekerleme*, a kind of nonsense poem or nursery rhyme. At least five book-length poems have survived, along with other spiritual treatises. Kaygusuz's work was first printed in Turkey in 1533.

Koyunoğlu (17th c.)

The real identity and life story of this Bektashi poet are uncertain. He may be related to another poet named Koyun Abdal. We know that he lived in the seventeenth-century and worked as a secretary within the Janissary administration. He died in 1645. His passionate and heartfelt *nefes'es* are still sung in Bektashi rituals.

Kul Himmet (16th c.)

Born in Tokat in central Turkey, Kul Himmet seems to have been a friend or student of Pir Sultan Abdal in the sixteenth-century. After Pir Sultan Abdal was hanged in 1590, Kul Himmet and his friends went into a long period of hiding. Kul Himmet was influenced by Shah Hatayi and Pir Sultan Abdal and influenced many Alevi-Bektashi poets in turn. His poems often indicate the rules and ways of the Sufi path and emphasize the "trinity" of Allah, Muhammad, and Ali. Kul Himmet was devoted to the idea of the Divine expressed through humanity.

Muhittin Abdal (16thc.)

Muhittin Abdal is one of the most original and strong-voiced of Bektashi poets. He seems to have lived in the Balkans in the sixteenth-century and to have been a student of a shaikh affiliated with both Hurufi and Kalenderi sects. The *tekke* he was involved with later became Bektashi, but Muhittin preserved strong Hurufi convictions in his work. Muhittin was most likely influenced poetically by Nesimi and Yunus Emre and wrote most of his *nefes'es* in the folk style called *hece*. Sometimes described as a "man of action," he traveled extensively, legend has it, during his long life.

Nesimi (14–15th c.)

Nesimi was skinned to death for his heresy in Aleppo in 1404. There is some disagreement about the identity of this very important poet of the fourteenth century. The scholar Gölpinarli assumes Nesimi used "Kul Nesimi" as a pen name. Özmen writes that there are in fact two Nesimis, one in the fourteenth century and one in the seventeenth century. Most sources indicate that his real name was Seyyid Imadeddin Nesimi and that he was born in the town of Nesim near Baghdad. Nesimi was educated in Arabic and Persian, as well as in mystical doctrines.

He is considered one of the seven great immortal poets of the Alevi-Bektashi tradition. Some sources indicate that he became the student, son-in-law, and successor of the legendary Fazlullah, the founder of the Hurufi sect of dervishes. Fazlullah claimed to be a prophet, and his followers felt he was the incarnation of Allah. These beliefs were enough to ensure that Tamerlane order his execution. While Bektashism differs significantly from Hurufism, Hurufism shows great appreciation for Ali and believes in the human being as divine; therefore, Nesimi was claimed by Bektashis as one of their own. Nesimi's beautiful lyrical poems were directly in line with the "An-al Haqq" (I am Truth) ideology of al-Hallaj. His poetry celebrates and deifies the human beloved. Hurufi doctrines hold that God is revealed in the face of the human being. Each feature has a meaning and symbolic value. The poems of Nesimi express these ideas.

Niyazi Mısri (1616-1694)

Known for his passionate writing and fearlessness, Niyazi Mısri's *ilahis* (devotional songs) are sung in the *tekkes* of many dervish orders and sometimes considered second only to those of Yunus Emre. Misri was born in Malatya, Turkey. He kindly wrote his own life story, so we have more details about him than is usual for Sufi poets. A member of the Halveti Dervish Order, he was a student of the great Ümmi Sinan. He came from a spiritually prominent family; his father was a *sheikh* in the Naqshbandi Order. At twenty-three, Misri began his search for a spiritual teacher, traveling extensively and eventually living in Egypt for three years. Guided by dreams, he finally came, at age thirty, to Ümmi Sinan. Ümmi Sinan trained him for nine years.

In 1656, he was made the *sheikh* of the Istanbul Tekke, and later established a *tekke* in Bursa. Apparently, he also worked as a candle maker and was married three times. However, his life had its share of tumult. He was exiled three times by the orthodox religious authorities who didn't like his ideologies and particular practices.

During Misri's time, for instance, the Sufi practice of *zikr* (repetition of the Divine names) and other dervish rituals were outlawed by the Ottoman sultan. To make matters worse, Misri often openly criticized the corruption of the government and officials in addition to speaking on spiritual matters, hoping to motivate reform within the palace and administration of Sultan Mehmet IV. For this, he was exiled to the isle of Rhodes, south of Greece. During his nine months there, his guard became his disciple.

When Misri returned to Bursa after the exile, instead of becoming less outspoken he became more so, claiming that Hasan and Husseyn (the sons of Ali) were prophets, a very radical claim. For these new claims he was exiled again, this time to Limni in the Aegean Sea. During the fifteen years of this second exile, his stature and influence grew. The Ottoman administration finally had to acknowledge the power of his followers to avoid a rebellion. However, Misri was poisoned in 1694, either for his political influence or the heterodoxy of his spirituality.

In one of his books, Misri writes in a remarkably tolerant and universalist spirit: "Whoever goes beyond appearances reaches the universe of the Friend, where all the saints, prophets and perfect beings reside. For those who aren't there yet, there is the Path (we call them Halveti, Khadiri, Mevlevi, etc.). There are as many paths as there are breaths of living creatures. Don't think one is higher than the other, or prefer one seeker over another."

Pir Sultan Abdal (16th c.)

One of the giants of Turkish folk poetry, Pir Sultan Abdal was a mystic, a poet, and a political leader. Using the imagery of the Anatolian landscape and standing firmly in the tradition of martyr-mystic al-Hallaj, Pir Sultan Abdal is considered one of the seven great Knowers of Truth by Alevis. Given the name Haydar by his parents, he was born in Sivas in central Turkey during the time of Shah Tahmasb (son of Shah Hatayi) of the Safavid Dynasty. The Safavids were the archenemy of the Ottoman state. In the sixteenth century, Pir Sultan Abdal led a rebellion against the Ottoman state, lost, and was imprisoned. Upon his refusal to give up his beliefs, he was hanged. Pir Sultan Abdal not only criticized social and political injustices but took action to correct the wrongs he saw. His poetry has been recited and his name invoked in almost every social struggle in Turkey for the past 500 years.

Riza Tevfik (1868–1948)

Known in Turkish literature as "Philosopher Riza," this poet's full name was Riza Tevfik Bolukbaşi. Born in 1868 in Edirne in the Balkans, he trained as a medical doctor but later became a professor of philosophy at Istanbul University. He served as minister of education and head of Parliament. He published many books and articles and wrote many commentaries on dervish poets and their poetry. An initiate of the Bektashi Order, Riza later became a Bektashi *baba*. Some of his poetry was composed to be used in Bektashi rituals. His collection of poems is entitled *Mirage of My Life*.

Şair Eşref (1847–1912)

Born in Manisa in western Turkey in 1847, his name literally means "Poet Esref." He is remembered mostly for his satirical poetry, which criticized corruption in the Ottoman state and addressed many of the social ills of his time. Educated at religious universities, he was a local governor during the Ottoman Empire. He became a Bektashi through Ruhi Baba, who initiated him into the order. Due to his poems, he spent at least a year in prison and time in exile. He wrote six books, including a collection (*divan*).

Seyyid Seyfullah Nizamoğlu (16th c.)

This poet was a *murshid* in the Halveti Order of dervishes. The title Seyyid indicates that he is descended from Ali. Nizamoğlu gained acclaim as a poet during the reign of Sultan Murad III in the sixteenth century. In his didactic poems, he criticized the orthodoxy, corruption, and materialism of his time. Nizamoğlu was well educated in both Islamic Law (*sharia*) and the Sufi path. He wrote in both folk and classical styles of poetry, and one can feel both the influence of Nesimi and Yunus Emre in his poems. Some of his poems were composed as *ilahi's* (devotional songs) and have been recited during *zikr* ceremonies for the last 500 years in Turkey.